Egyptian
Mummies

Carol Andrews

Published for The Trustees of

The British Museum by

BRITISH MUSEUM  PRESS

Published by British Museum Press
A division of The British Museum
Company Ltd
46 Bloomsbury Street
London WC1B 3QQ

First published 1984
Second edition 1998

A catalogue record for this book is
available from the British Library

ISBN 0-7141-2139-8

Designed by Martin Richards
Series design by Carroll Associates

Typeset in Van Dijck

Manufactured in Hong Kong by
Imago

Front cover *Mummy of man wearing
gilded and painted cartonnage mummy
mask and separate cover for abdomen and
legs beneath linen cross-straps. First
century* BC *to first century* AD.
Height 1.63 m (5 ft 4 $^{1}/_{2}$ in).

Back cover *Underside of
wooden coffin of Itineb with
animated* djed *representing
Osiris and sun-god's barque.
Twenty-sixth Dynasty, c.600* BC.
Height 1.83 m (6 ft).

Right *Wooden coffin and mummy of
unnamed Theban priestess. Twenty-first
Dynasty, c.100* BC. *Height 1.83 m
(6 ft).*

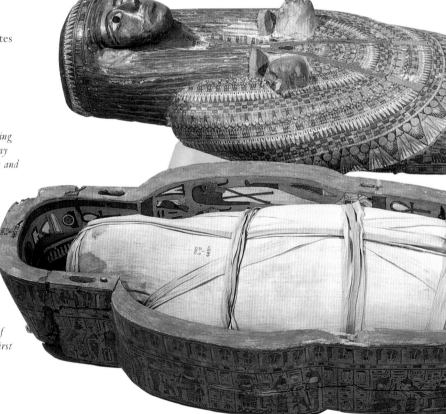

Contents

Chapter One | Why Mummies?

Ginger is an ancient Egyptian who died more than five thousand years ago yet his hair, which gives him his nick-name, and even his toe- and finger-nails have been perfectly preserved. He lacks only the top joint of one of his forefingers which mysteriously vanished from the British Museum over a weekend in March 1900, within twenty-four hours of the body first being unpacked. Disappointingly, recent examination has led to its rediscovery, clutched tightly in his fist. Like most Egyptians of the Predynastic Period (before 3100 BC) Ginger was buried, wrapped only in skins or matting, in a shallow grave in the desert sand at the edge of the cultivation. Hot dry sand absorbs the water which constitutes 75% by weight of the human body and without which bacteria cannot breed and cause decay. So Ginger has survived lying curled up on his left side, gaunt and shrunken but recognisable.

The location of a roughly-marked desert grave was soon lost and Egyptians of a later period must sometimes have uncovered unexpectedly the sand-dried corpse of an ancestor. Yet the lifelike appearance of such bodies may not have given rise to the Egyptian belief in an afterlife: an expectation of survival already existed when Ginger was buried, for he took with him his flint knives for use in the other world and black-topped red pots in which to store food and drink for the long journey there. Wealthier burials of the same period contain combs of bone or ivory, jewellery and stone palettes on which to grind eye-paint. Because he died before the advent of writing, the form of afterlife which Ginger expected to enjoy can only be guessed, but in the historic period it was believed that various spirits were released at death, of which the most important were the *Ka*, the *Ba* and the *Akh*.

1 *'Ginger', a Predynastic man whose body was preserved naturally by the hot dry sand in which he was buried. The heat of the sand absorbed the moisture without which bacteria cannot breed and cause decay. Gebelein. Naqada II Period, c.3200 BC. Unflexed length 1.63 m (5 ft 4 in).*

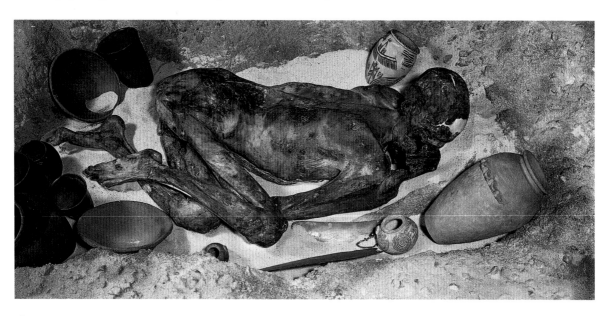

The *Ka*, represented symbolically by two upstretched human arms, was the vital life-force or genius. It was created at the same time as a man's physical body, which it resembled in every respect, but had no separate existence of its own until after death. Indeed, the expression 'to go to one's *Ka*' meant 'to die'. Within the tomb, sometimes called House of the *Ka*, it was free to move between the burial chamber, the funerary statue and the offering place. It was the *Ka* which inhabited the statue of the deceased, watching for the time to emerge through the False Door to eat and drink the essence of the offerings which were presented daily at the tomb. The close connection between the *Ka* and its essential food supplies can be gauged by the fact that in Egyptian the plural of the word *Ka* means 'sustenance'.

The human-headed *Ba*-bird was far more versatile. It could take any form it wished in order to revisit the world of the living or travel across the sky in the sun-god's boat, though it always eventually returned to the tomb. The title of Chapter 89 of the *Book of the Dead* – 'Spell to allow a *Ba* to be reunited with its corpse in the necropolis' – shows the tie which existed between this wandering spirit and the body in the burial chamber. It was also the *Ba* which anxiously witnessed the weighing of its master's heart in the Underworld in case the result prevented entry into the Egyptian paradise. *Ba* is sometimes translated as 'soul' but the term did not convey this meaning to the Copts (whose language is that of the hieroglyphs, although written with Greek letters) for they preferred to use instead the Greek word 'psyche'. The *Ba* perhaps embodied the characteristics or personality of a man, the individual traits which distinguished him from all other human beings.

2 Vignette from the funerary papyrus of Nesitanebtasheru showing the deceased seated before a standard upon which upraised arms, symbolising the Ka, *embrace food offerings. Thebes. Twenty-first Dynasty, c.965 BC. Height 7.7 cm (3 1/16 in).*

5

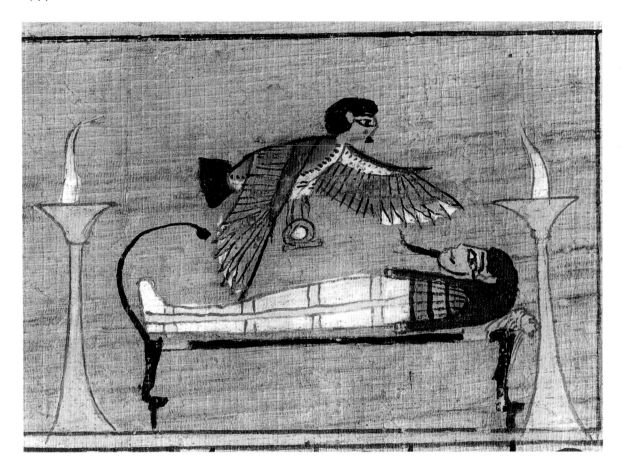

3 Vignette illustrating Chapter 89 of the Book of the Dead *of the scribe Any: a spell to unite the* Ba *with its mummy. Nineteenth Dynasty, c.1250 BC. Height 7 cm (2 ³/₄ in).*

The crested ibis represented pictorially a man's *Akh* or immortality. This most unearthly of spirits severed all ties with the mortal remains in order to join the cold and imperishable stars. In Coptic the word derived from *Akh* can sometimes mean 'ghost'.

Although the *Ka, Ba* and *Akh* were spirits, it was believed that the preservation of the physical body in a recognisable form was essential if they too were to survive. As long as the dead were buried in the sand as Ginger had been, and as the poorer classes continued to be throughout much of Egypt's history, the chances of natural preservation were good. Ironically, it was the bodies of the wealthy and powerful which suffered most through being placed inside coffins in specially prepared underground burial chambers lined with wood, mud-brick or even stone. In these damp, sandless conditions bodies quickly rotted and the most basic Egyptian belief, that an afterlife required survival of the corpse, was threatened. At first, during the Early Dynastic Period, in a vain attempt to counteract the almost complete loss of flesh resulting from the exclu-

4 Detail of the inside decoration of the wooden outer coffin of Seni, a physician, with a hieroglyphic representation of the Akh-*bird, a crested ibis. El-Bersha. Twelfth Dynasty, c.1900 BC. Height 15 cm (5 ⁹/₁₀ in).*

sion of sand, bodies were tightly wrapped in strips of resin-soaked linen before being placed inside a coffin. All this did was to preserve a hollow shell of bandages which retained the original shape of the corpse but contained only a loose jumble of bones. By the Third Dynasty an effective means of preserving bodies artificially was being sought.

The Egyptian process of artificially preserving the dead is termed embalming or mummification. The word 'embalm' comes from the Latin words meaning '(to put) into aromatic resins', quite an accurate description because bodies were anointed with unguents, resins and oils. 'Mummify' comes from the Arabic word *mummiya* meaning bitumen or pitch, and arose from a misunderstanding: badly embalmed bodies of the Late Period (after 600 BC) were filled with molten resin which impregnated the very bones. It was their blackened and brittle appearance which suggested that they had been dipped in bitumen and their good burning qualities which seemed to confirm it. Wallis Budge, one-time Keeper of the Egyptian Collection, graphically describes how 'the arms, legs, hands, and feet of such mummies break with a sound like the cracking of chemical glass tubing, they burn very freely and give out great heat.'

The Egyptians were aware that putrefaction started in the abdomen so an essential step was the removal of the internal organs. Not only did this allow the empty body cavity to be treated, but it also meant the dehydrating process could be carried out more effectively from inside and out simultaneously. Bodies from which the internal organs have been removed are not hunched-up: to provide easier access to the internal organs the corpse was stretched out and it was in this position that it was buried.

Mummification was practised from at least the early Fourth Dynasty (about 2600 BC), judging from the remains of the internal organs of Queen Hetepheres which were still within their Canopic chest when her burial was discovered at Giza. Curiously, her body seems not to have been interred at the same time. Once established, mummification continued in use until the early Coptic Period, a span of nearly three thousand years, although by the end it was a pale shadow of what it had been at its peak during the Twenty-first Dynasty (1070–945 BC). Over so long a period the quality of treatment varied considerably and even royalty itself was not exempt from indifferent embalming. Of all mummies those of Yuya and Thuya, Tutankhamun's great-grandparents, are perhaps the most perfectly preserved, yet the body of Tutankhamun himself was virtually carbonised through chemical interreaction of the materials used by the embalmers.

5 Unwrapped mummy of an elderly woman unusually well-embalmed for the time when bodies were more often completely impregnated with molten resin, their appearance giving rise to the term 'mummy' from the Arabic word meaning 'bitumen'. Late Period, after 600 BC. Length 1.52 m (5 ft).

Although burial in the sand dried out a body, the skin became a baked membrane stretched tightly over the skeletal frame and, if flicked with a finger-nail, gave out a sound like a wooden drum being rapped. A dehydrating agent was needed which would leave the body more flexible and lifelike. Such a material was natron, a natural compound of sodium carbonate and bicarbonate with admixtures of sodium sulphate and chloride, which was found crystallised in considerable quantities along the edges of the lakes in the Wadi Natrun, forty miles north-west of Cairo. Like hot dry sand natron absorbs water, and is also mildly antiseptic: in Egyptian one of its names is *neteryt*, meaning 'belonging to the god', probably because it was used as early as the Old Kingdom as a ritual purifier. Priests even chewed pellets of it during religious ceremonies. Such an association made natron a particularly suitable material for treating the bodies of the deified dead.

At first, natron may have been used in solution rather than as dry crystals. The linen packages containing Queen Hetepheres' internal organs were still soaking in a 3% solution of natron when they were found, yet it has been established subsequently that so weak a concentration is insufficient to prevent decay. This suggests that the queen's viscera had already been treated and that the natron solution was merely a preservative. Experiments have shown that natron in a concentrated solution can dehydrate, but that the time required is far greater than

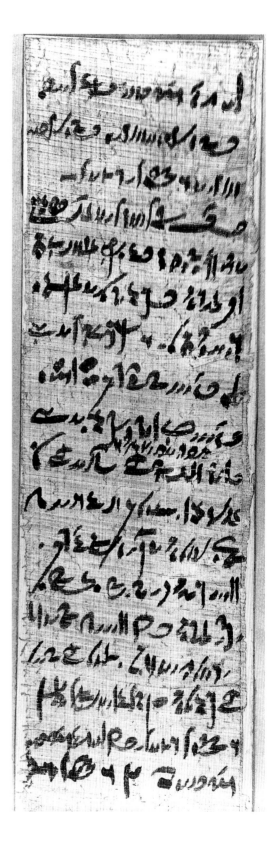

when dry crystals are used. Perhaps in this fact lies the answer to the curious case of Queen Meresankh III, whose embalming treatment took 272 days, some four times longer than usual. The hieroglyphic inscription at the entrance to her tomb at Giza stating that '[in] year 1, first month of the summer season, day 21, her *Ka* rested, she went to the *wabt* [embalming place]; year 2, second month of the spring season, day 18, she went to her beautiful tomb' has caused much puzzlement but could be explained if natron in solution had been used. On the other hand, large containers would be necessary to soak fully-grown bodies, yet no trace of even one such salt bath has ever been found. A further argument against the use of fluid natron, except in the earliest period of experimentation, is the daunting prospect which a very soggy corpse would have presented to those in charge of the bandaging.

The use of natron in solution, combined with the original restriction of embalming to royalty and favoured courtiers, perhaps explains why there are only a handful of complete mummies of Old Kingdom date still in existence. There used to be one at the Royal College of Surgeons in London, but it was destroyed during an air-raid in 1941, a four-thousand-year-old casualty of World War II. One of the oldest mummies to survive is that of Waty, found at Saqqara in the tomb of a court singer called Nefer, and dating to the late Fifth Dynasty, about 2400 BC. Waty has been so tightly and expertly wrapped in resin-soaked bandages that his features can be discerned clearly through the linen; even a callus on the sole of one foot is noticeable. Details of his eyes, eyebrows and moustache, picked out in black paint add to the lifelike effect.

For the next twenty-five centuries the Egyptians carried out the embalming process with varying degrees of success on an ever-increasing

7 (Opposite left) The excellently embalmed body of king Sety I, found in the royal cache of mummies at Deir el-Bahri, Thebes, and virtually undamaged by ancient tomb robbers. Nineteenth Dynasty, c.1274 BC. Height 1.66 m (5 ft 5 1/2 in). (Cairo Museum.)

8 (Opposite right) Demotic letter from an embalmer, acknowledging receipt of natron and linen and promising to hand over the embalmed body on the 72nd day. Thebes. December 270 to January 269 BC. Height 20 cm (14 7/8 in).

9 Waty, one of the earliest surviving mummies, in situ in the tomb of Nefer at Saqqara where he was found. Fifth Dynasty, c.2400 BC.

number of their dead. Yet, apart from some badly damaged Theban tomb scenes showing the final bandaging, they have left no pictorial record of its early stages, possibly because they considered it too sacred a subject to be represented. There are only two very late papyri containing a text which has been called 'The Ritual of Embalming'. Neither papyrus is earlier in date than the first century AD but their common source is undoubtedly a much earlier document, a kind of embalmer's hand-book. It must have laid down for the embalmer every move to be made towards the corpse, every material required and exactly how to use it. Even the appropriate ritual utterance to accompany every action was specified. Unfortunately both papyri lack a beginning, and what is left concerns the final stages of the process: the anointings of the body, the placing of the treated internal organs within the Canopic jars and the bandaging of the mummy.

There does exist, however, an eyewitness account of mummification, written by a foreigner. When the Greek historian Herodotus visited Egypt shortly after 450 BC the art of embalming was well past its peak but he was an accurate recorder of what he plainly thought a very quaint Egyptian custom. Of embalming Herodotus writes:

'There are those who are established in this profession and who practise the craft. When a corpse is carried in to them they show the bearers wooden models of mummies, painted in exact imitation of the real thing. The best method of embalming, so they say, is that which was practised on one whose name I cannot mention in this context [i.e. Osiris, the god of the dead]. The second method they demonstrate is somewhat inferior and costs less. The third is cheapest of all. Having indicated the differences, they ask by which method the corpse is to be prepared. And when the bearers have agreed a price and departed, the embalmers, left behind in the workshop, begin embalming.

'In the best treatment, first of all they draw out the brains through the nostrils with an iron hook. When they have removed what they can in this way they flush out the remainder with drugs. Next they make an incision in the-flank with a sharp obsidian blade through which they extract all the internal organs. Then they clean out the body cavity, rinsing it with palm wine and pounded spices, all except frankincense, and stitching it up again. And when they have done this they cover the corpse with natron for seventy days, but for no longer, and so mummify it. After the seventy days are up they wash the corpse and wrap it from head to toe in bandages of the finest linen anointed with gum, which the Egyptians use for the most part instead of glue. Finally they hand over the body to the relatives who place it in a wooden coffin in the shape of a man before shutting it up in a burial chamber, propped upright against a wall. This is the most costly method of preparing the dead.

'Those for whom the second and less expensive way has been chosen are treated as follows: the embalmers fill their syringes with cedar oil which they inject into the abdomen, neither cutting the flesh nor extracting the internal organs but introducing the oil through the anus which is then stopped up. Then they mummify the body for the prescribed number of days, at the end of which they allow the oil which had been injected to escape. So great is its strength that it brings away all the internal organs in liquid form. Moreover the natron eats away the flesh, reducing the body to skin and bone. After they have done this the embalmers give back the body without further ado.

'The third method of embalming which is practised upon the bodies of the poor is this: the embalmers wash out the abdomen with a purge, mummify the corpse for seventy days then give it back to be taken away.'

So ends Herodotus' account of the embalming process, but he cannot refrain from a final titbit of rather malicious gossip:

'Now the wives of important men, when they die, are not handed over to be embalmed at once, nor women who are especially beautiful or famous. Not until the third or fourth day has elapsed are they given to the embalmers. They do this to prevent the embalmers violating the corpse. For they say that one of them was caught who had actually abused a newly-dead woman; a workmate denounced him.'

It is true that a surprising number of bodies, especially of Middle Kingdom and Late Period date, suffered considerable decomposition before being treated but the incidence is as great in male mummies as in female! However, there must have been times, during an epidemic or after civil disturbances, when the embalmers were kept too busy to deal with every corpse immediately it was brought to them. On the other hand, especially at the time when Herodotus was writing, embalming was just another industry and those involved with the most menial aspects of the treatment did not enjoy the prestige nor the rank of earlier practitioners. Given these conditions such an atrocity could have taken place, but Herodotus' version does smack of scandal-mongering and a story whose salient points have become more outrageous with each retelling.

Examination of mummies and experiments with the bodies of rats and birds have subsequently proved that Herodotus is a more trustworthy source than used to be thought. In particular, his rather precise description of how natron was used is now known to be correct. Because he wrote in Greek and the Greeks did not embalm their dead he had to adapt an existing Greek word which in context would mean 'mummify'. The word he uses actually means 'to dry-salt fish', not pickle or marinate but dry-salt, and nowhere in his account does he speak of 'steeping' bodies in natron. The first modern author to have mistranslated the relevant passage in this way seems to have been Thomas Pettigrew.

Pettigrew was a surgeon and antiquary whose chief claim to fame lay in vaccinating Queen Victoria and unwrapping Egyptian mummies in public before large and appreciative audiences. His methods were far from scientific. As he himself records of a mummy unwrapped on 6 April 1833: 'It was a task of no little difficulty and required considerable force to separate the layers of bandages from the body; levers were absolutely necessary.' A debt of gratitude is owed to the Trustees of the British Museum who refused to allow Pettigrew to unwrap any of the mummies in their collection when he applied 'to be permitted to examine one or two of the mummies contained in that *national* [Pettigrew's italics] establishment.' Their official reason was that it 'would destroy the integrity of the collection.' It is more likely they feared it would destroy the mummies!

When so well-known an authority as Pettigrew supported the idea that fluid natron was used in mummification dissenting views were largely ignored. The error was perpetuated by Wallis Budge in his hugely successful work, *The Mummy*, published in 1893, and for the next forty-five years or so it was not only accepted that the Egyptians desiccated their dead by soaking them in natron solution, but evidence was even produced to 'prove' it. Fluid natron, so it was said, caused the toe- and fingernails to become detached which was why so many mummies had them tied on with thread or, as in the case of Tutankhamun and King Psusennes, protected by gold stalls. It also removed the outer skin and body hair and, in extreme cases, detached the limbs from the trunk, hence the bodies with defective or overabundant limbs.

In fact, stalls for the toes and fingers were only put in place after the body had been treated and wrapped. Shrinkage caused by the dry natron treatment coupled with slight putrefaction would warrant the

10 *Gold finger and toe stalls, fitting over the embalmed digits before wrapping began. From the intact burial of Queen Takhut. Tell Atrib. Twenty-sixth Dynasty, c.590 BC. (Cairo Museum.)*

tying on of nails. More mummies than were realised retained their outer skin but it usually peeled off, stuck to the innermost bandages, and was destroyed when the wrappings were removed. As for those mummies in which the limbs are in complete disarray, lacking or too numerous to have belonged to one body alone, they date almost without exception to the Graeco-Roman Period (after 305 BC). By then embalmers paid less attention to the actual treatment of the body than to the external appearance of the wrappings. Indeed, some bodies of the period were in quite an advanced state of decomposition before receiving any attention and this would have caused the limbs to become detached. If a number of decaying bodies were buried in the same heap of natron and those in charge of the subsequent wrapping were careless about which, or indeed how many limbs were bandaged with each torso, such 'composite' mummies can readily be explained. So all the observations which used to be produced as evidence that natron in solution was the dehydrating agent can be discounted. It is, moreover, ironic that at a time when leading authorities were wilfully misunderstanding Herodotus, a customs official in Cairo, faced with the problem of levying tax on the royal mummies as they entered the city on their way to the Cairo Museum, decided to charge them under the category of dried fish!

The one important matter in which Herodotus has been proved inaccurate is the length of time devoted to the drying out of the corpse. Experiments have shown that after forty days the further decay of a body buried in natron is negligible, so to keep it drying out longer is pointless. The seventy days quoted by Herodotus almost certainly spanned the whole embalming process including the washings, anointings and bandaging after the drying out. Egyptian texts speak of the dead spending seventy days in the embalming tent and being placed in the coffin on the seventieth day after death. Day sixteen had some unknown significance, but probably marked the beginning of the drying out; on day thirty-five the wrapping began. The correct allocation of forty out of seventy days is recorded in the Book of Genesis, where it is written that when Jacob died, 'Joseph commanded his servants and physicians to embalm his father. And forty days were fulfilled for him, for so are fulfilled the days of those which are embalmed; and the Egyptians mourned for him for three score and ten days' (Genesis 50: 2, 3). In ritual matters every number had a particular significance for the Egyptians, so the specific time spent in the embalming place would not have been chosen without good reason. Perhaps it was connected with the period of seventy days during which the Dog Star Sirius, whose rising heralded the Egyptian New Year, could not be seen in the night sky. As the star 'died' and was reborn after seventy days, so the dead, after a similar period of treatment, would be ready for rebirth in the Other World.

Chapter Two | How Mummies Were Made

Information gathered from the examination of mummies and embalming materials and the results of experiments to test embalming methods have allowed the stages of the embalming process in its most developed form to be reconstructed in some detail.

Not long after death, because of the climate, the body was taken to the *ibu* or place of purification. Originally this was a temporary structure, possibly a tent, built on a T-shaped plan and with access to water. It would probably be located on the west bank of the Nile, as were most Egyptian cemeteries, because the west, where the sun set during its passage into the Underworld, was especially associated with the dead. It would also be sited as far away as possible from populated areas, although when the wind changed city-dwellers must often have been reminded forcibly of the place to which their own body would one day be borne. In the *ibu* the corpse was stripped and washed down with water in which natron had been dissolved. As a ritual act this washing symbolised the rebirth of the dead, just as the sun was reborn each day after bathing in the waters of the primordial ocean. On a more practical level, the antiseptic qualities of natron would have helped to keep the corpse sweet a little longer. A few representations of this ritual purification have survived painted on coffins or occasionally on tomb walls. Either the deceased appears as though still alive, kneeling on a mat or perched on a large pot while streams of water are poured from above or, more realistically, he is a blackened corpse, propped up on a mat or lying in a water-filled trough while more water cascades down from vessels held by attendants.

The actual embalming took place elsewhere, in the nearby *wabt* or *per nefer*, an enclosure within which stood a tent or booth. One of the titles of Anubis, the jackal-headed god of embalming, was 'the one in charge of the divine [i.e. embalming] booth' and he is often shown attending to the mummy as it lies within just such a light structure. For the Late Period (after 600 BC), when far greater numbers of bodies were embalmed, there is evidence that permanent mud-brick buildings, often of considerable size, housed the various stages of the process.

Herodotus and other classical authors mention only two classes of embalmer, but Egyptian sources show that the profession was highly organised on the same lines as a temple priesthood. The embalmers who supervised the process bore the highest priestly titles, presumably a survival from those early days when embalming was restricted to the bodies of royalty and highly favoured courtiers and only the highest officials were considered worthy to treat such exalted corpses. At the head of operations was the *hery seshta* or Controller of the Mysteries who represented Anubis; he may even have donned a jackal-headed mask at various important stages of the process in order to stress his identification with the god. His second in command was the *khetemu neter* or God's Seal-bearer, a title originally borne by priests of Osiris, the god whose body,

11 *Detail from the cartonnage inner coffin of the Theban priestess Tjentmutengebtyu showing the deceased as though still alive, kneeling on a mat while Horus and Thoth purify her with streams of* ankh *and* was *symbols instead of water. Twenty-second Dynasty, c.900 BC.*

12 *Scenes from the wooden coffin of Djedbastiufankh. Below: the blackened corpse purified by streams of water. Centre: the body buried in natron. Top left: the mummy and Canopic jars. Top right: Anubis attends the wrapped mummy. Late Period, after 600 BC. (Hildesheim Museum.)*

according to legend, was the first ever to be embalmed. Just as important was the *khery heb* or Lector Priest who read the appropriate instructions and magical utterances at every stage of the treatment and acted as scribe and bookkeeper. These officials supervised a small army of lesser technicians called *wetyw* or bandagers. Part of their job must indeed have included the rolling up of bandages and the wrapping of the body, but they also mixed unguents, carried about water and natron, washed the internal organs, heated up resin and carried out the thousand and one menial tasks required during the embalming process.

13 *Detail of vignette from the* Book of the Dead *of the scribe Any showing Anubis tending the mummy within the embalming booth. Nineteenth Dynasty, c.1250* BC. *Height 9.5 cm (3 ³/4 in).*

When the corpse arrived at the embalming place it was stretched out on four wooden blocks upon a wooden board. Just such an embalming board with blocks, found at Thebes, measures over 2.1 m (7 ft) in length and over 1.4 m (4 ½ ft) in width: its discoverer remarked on its ghoulish resemblance to a modern dissecting table. Because of the heat, the first priority was preservation of the features, so probably the head was coated with molten resin at the earliest opportunity. Until the early Eighteenth Dynasty (about 1500 BC), the brain was usually left untouched, but after this date it became standard practice in the best treatment to extract it. First, a pointed instrument was pushed up a nostril to break through the ethmoid bone into the cranium. Then a rod with hooked or curled end was poked up and swished around inside the skull to slice up the brain and allow it to be removed piecemeal. Sometimes the fragments were spooned out by means of a rod with a cupped end; very occasionally the brain was extracted through an eye-socket or a hole made in the skull. But no matter how it was removed it was never preserved; the fragments were just thrown away. Finally, the empty skull was filled with sawdust, resin or resin-soaked linen introduced through the hole by which the brain had been extracted. Perhaps it was the molten resin being introduced into the empty cranium which Herodotus misinterpreted as purging drugs to dissolve the brain.

Next, in the most developed treatment, the embalmer drew out the stomach and intestines through an incision in the lower abdomen. By

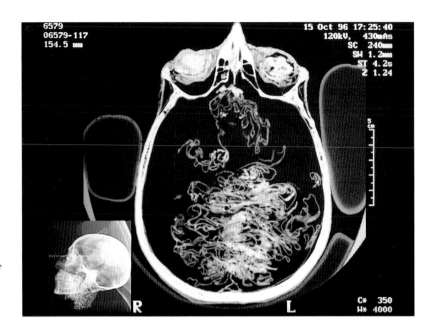

14 Below and right *Head of an unknown male mummy with inlaid eye and* CAT-*scan of the same head, showing the strips of linen used to stuff the empty cranium. About 1000* BC.

puncturing the diaphragm, he was able to pull out the lungs and liver too but he never deliberately removed the heart: as the seat of the intelligence it was always left inside the body cavity; sometimes it was even stitched in place after accidental removal. It was considered so important that heart and body be kept together that no less than three spells in the *Book of the Dead*, Chapters 27, 28 and 29, were entitled 'To prevent the heart being taken away from a man in the necropolis'. The kidneys were sometimes removed, but more often than not they were left in place. The fact that no word for them in Egyptian has been identified with complete certainty suggests that their occasional extraction was accidental: the Egyptians did not realise they were there!

Before the later Eighteenth Dynasty the internal organs were not always removed, even in the case of royalty who could have expected the best treatment available. Some of the mummies of great court ladies who were buried beneath the mortuary temple of King Mentuhotep II at Deir el-Bahri (about 2020 BC) had no embalming incision, just as in the second method recounted by Herodotus. But there the similarity ended, for when they were opened up the body cavity was found still to contain the shrivelled remains of the internal organs. Of course, these bodies were treated before the embalming process had been perfected whereas Herodotus was describing a method in use sixteen centuries later. But the accuracy of his account is confirmed by two mummies of the Persian

Period, the very time when he was writing. They carry no embalming incision yet they lack their internal organs which could only have been extracted *per anum*. On the other hand, his reference to the use of 'oil of cedar' is curious, for juniper oil, as it is usually identified, does not have the purging qualities which Herodotus ascribes to it. However, an Egyptologist and chemist called Lucas, who carried out much important research into the embalming process, discovered that if a corpse was buried in natron while it still contained its internal organs they turned into a dark brown sludge. Perhaps when Herodotus saw the results of this natural dissolution he supposed it had to be caused by the introduction of a dissolving agent, his 'oil of cedar'.

Diodorus Siculus, a Greek historian who wrote about embalming some four hundred years after Herodotus, adds details missing in the earlier account. He says that the incision was made in the left flank and in nearly every mummy examined which bears an embalming incision it is indeed on the left side. Both he and Herodotus agree that the blade used to make the incision was of Ethiopian stone, or obsidian. Throughout Egypt's history this glass-like material had to be imported and, in addition, seems only to have been worked into blades during the Predynastic Period. On the other hand, flint knives continued to be used for ritual purposes, such as circumcision, long after metal blades were common. Perhaps the continued use of obsidian was an ancient survival hallowed by tradition. One curious point made only by Diodorus is that the man who made the incision, the 'ripper-up' as the Greek text graphically describes him, had at once to take to his heels attended by curses and even stones from those present. 'Because', as Diodorus explains, 'they suppose him to be worthy of hatred who applies force to the corpse of a fellow creature, or wounds it, or executes any evil in general upon it.' Presumably this was another ritual survival, probably from an ancient law which accounted it a sin to injure a dead body in any way.

Herodotus gives no information about what happened to the internal organs after they were extracted; Diodorus merely adds that they were rinsed in palm wine and spices to sweeten them. In fact, like the corpse itself, they were dried out in natron. When they had been completely dehydrated they were rinsed, dried, anointed with sweet-smelling ointments and coated in molten resin before being wrapped in

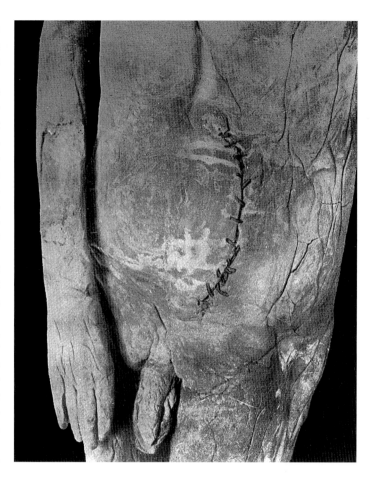

15 *Unwrapped male mummy showing the embalming incision on the left side. Usually the lips of the wound were merely drawn together beneath the embalming plate; here they have been sewn together with crude tacking stitches. Twenty-first Dynasty, c.1000 BC. (Cairo Museum.)*

yards of linen bandages into four separate packages. Ideally, one package contained the liver, another the lungs, a third the stomach and the last the intestines. The linen-wrapped internal organs of Queen Hetepheres were in a plain alabaster chest compartmented into four; for royalty at least stone containers were probably always used. Tutankhamun's internal organs were also stored in an alabaster box, but this was shrine-shaped and elaborately decorated with appropriate spells, amuletic signs and figures of protecting goddesses. In addition, each of the compartments had a human-headed stopper and each linen package was enclosed in a miniature gold mummy case inlaid with semiprecious stones and glass, an exact replica of the second coffin in which the king himself lay. Five hundred years later, when King Heqakheperre Sheshonq was buried at Tanis, his internal organs were also placed inside four miniature coffins, this time of silver, the material from which his full-sized coffin was made.

Roughly carved stone vessels with flat lids, occasionally still in sets of four, have survived from some non-royal burials of Old Kingdom date. They never show signs of use but that is hardly surprising considering the experimental state of embalming at the time. There can be no doubt, however, that they are the forerunners of the sets of four jars with human-headed stoppers in which the internal organs were stored from at least the time of the early Middle Kingdom, about 2000 BC. Early

16 *An early set of Canopic jars, belonging to the physician Gua, in their wooden Canopic chest. The vessels are made of alabaster but the stoppers, all human-headed, are made of wood. El-Bersha. Twelfth Dynasty, c.1900 BC. 54.7 cm square (21 9/16 in square).*

Egyptologists rather mistakenly called them Canopic jars because they seemed to resemble the form under which Canopus, pilot of King Menelaus, was said to have been worshipped in the Egyptian delta. The quaint connection between the husband of Helen of Troy, a Greek sailor, an Egyptian city and a curiously-shaped pot was made by certain Classical authors attempting to explain a fetish worshipped in the neighbourhood of the city they called Canopus. Actually, it represented Osiris, the god of the dead, but their explanation is far more colourful. Helen and Menelaus, so they said, were returning to Greece at the end of

17 *Wooden Canopic chest on a sled, containing wooden Canopic jars made for a man called Nebi, decorated with figures of the Canopic deities and protective goddesses. Eighteenth Dynasty, c.1500 BC. 53 cm square (20 7/8 in square).*

the Trojan War when they were driven off course to the shores of Egypt by a terrible storm in which Canopus perished. He was buried near the delta city which henceforth bore his name, and it was he who was revered in the vicinity under the form of a human-headed jar with a foot and swollen belly.

Canopic jars were usually stored within the compartments of a wooden chest which was clearly looked upon as a coffin for the mummified internal organs. Many Canopic boxes are decorated in the same way as the full-sized coffin in which their owner lay. The parallel was even more clearly drawn during the early Middle Kingdom when the linen packages were sometimes fitted with miniature mummy masks just as the mummy itself now wore a mask over its head and shoulders. Canopic jars could be made from stone, cartonnage, pottery, glazed composition, wood or a combination of these materials. Early sets in particular were often of stone with painted wooden heads, but by the Late Period (after 600 BC) different materials may have been combined in a deliberate attempt to deceive: in some sets the stoppers are indeed of stone but the bodies are of pottery cunningly painted to imitate stone. It would be interesting to know whether the embalmers charged the grieving relatives the cost of jars made entirely of stone, or whether it was the family itself who cut the costs of the burial equipment.

The contents of Canopic jars were placed under the protection of four minor gods called the Sons of Horus or, because of their specialised duties, the Canopic deities. Imsety looked after the liver, Hapy the lungs, Duamutef the stomach and Qebhsenuef the intestines. As an additional safeguard they were also linked with four powerful goddesses, Isis, Nephthys, Neith and Selkit respectively. After the late Eighteenth Dynasty, the stoppers of the jars were always shaped like the heads of the Sons of Horus. Imsety's jar was still human-headed but Hapy's had the head of a baboon, Duamutef's a jackal and Qebhsenuef's a falcon.

During the Twenty-first Dynasty for some unknown reason it became the practice to return the linen packages containing the internal organs to their relevant positions within the body cavity, along with wax or clay figures of the Sons of Horus to give them protection. Yet a full set of Canopic jars continued to be provided. During the Twenty-sixth Dynasty too, and especially the Ptolemaic Period, when the packages

18 *Brightly painted wooden dummy Canopic jars for an unnamed person, the stoppers representing the heads of the Canopic deities. Twenty-first Dynasty, c.1000 BC Height of Imsety 31 cm (12 ¹/₅ in).*

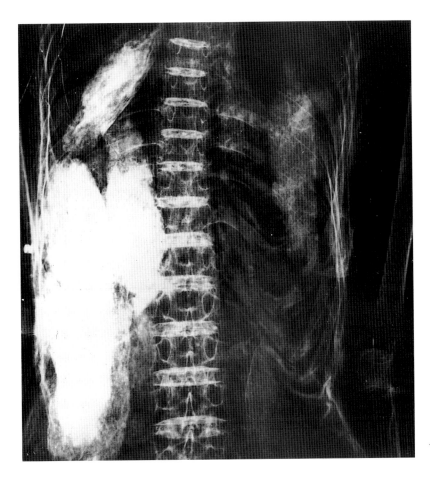

19 *X-ray of the chest of an elderly woman's mummy showing the linen packages containing the internal organs. Late Period, after 600 BC.*

were usually wrapped between the mummy's legs, Canopic jars were still part of the burial equipment, although they were often dummies which had not been hollowed out. It seems that by this late date the presence of Canopic jars had become characteristic of what was considered a good burial so they continued to be provided even when changing embalming practices meant that they were no longer strictly necessary.

Meanwhile, for the body itself, the next step was dehydration. First, the empty chest cavity and abdomen were rinsed out with a sterilising agent, possibly palm wine and spices as Herodotus suggests. This stage has left no traces in surviving mummies but would have been very necessary for deodorant reasons. Before the body was placed in natron it was repacked with temporary stuffing to help speed up the drying out process and also prevent accidental crushing and disfigurement. Rags, straw, wood shavings, sand, dried grass, anything which came to hand was crammed inside. Linen bags filled with natron were also used as temporary stuffing, placed nearest the inner surface to carry on the drying out process from within. Perhaps, as Herodotus records, aromatic resins or spices were introduced too; but whatever measures were taken to allay it, the stench in the embalmers' workshop must by now have been truly appalling.

During its dehydration the body was heaped over with natron while lying stretched out on a low stone table which sloped slightly from head to foot to aid drainage. Surviving examples of embalming tables, like those used at Memphis during the mummifcation of the Apis bulls, are slightly concave with a small reservoir at one end to catch the fluids which drained from the body. Along the two longer sides was usually carved an elongated lion in profile, probably to create the illusion that the corpse was sleeping on a lion-form bed. Bodies of less wealthy clients may have been dumped on matting laid on the ground. But whether on low table or mat, corpses heaped over with natron would not be under constant supervision during the forty days it took to dry them out, and this fact probably accounts for those mummies which lack a limb or two: it must have been easy for a jackal or pariah dog to slink in at night and carry off a well-salted trophy.

20 *Alabaster embalming table, in situ at Memphis, used during the drying-out in natron of the Apis bulls. The longer sides, sloping slightly from head to foot, are carved in imitation of a lion-form bier; the top surface is concave and a container caught the fluids which drained from the corpse during treatment. Late Dynastic Period, c.350 BC.*

At the end of forty days in natron the body was a ghastly sight. It was much darker in colour and up to 75% lighter in weight. The arms and legs were like matchsticks but the trunk was sleeved in loose, rather rubbery skin, for most of the muscles and soft tissues had been broken down or dissolved. The abdomen, however, was abnormally swollen and the skin over it taut. Now the embalmer needed to practise all his art to restore the deceased to as lifelike an appearance as possible. First the temporary stuffing was removed, but not discarded: whether putrid swabs, stained linen pads or soggy bags of natron, everything which had come into contact with the body during treatment was saved, stored in pots, to be buried during the funeral. These refuse embalming materials had soaked up vital body fluids and, moreover, contained fragments of skin, hair, nails, all of which were required by the deceased in the Other World. Just as important, not even a single hair could be allowed to fall into the wrong hands in case, in an enemy's possession, it gave him the power to bewitch the dead.

After the corpse had been rinsed out, washed down and thoroughly dried to prevent mould forming it was ready to be restuffed permanently. Wads of linen or linen soaked with resin, bags of natron crystals, of sawdust or sawdust mixed with resin were all used on occasion to pack the body cavity, although King Siptah of the Nineteenth Dynasty, King Ramesses IV of the Twentieth Dynasty and a private person of Twenty-first Dynasty date had to make do with dried lichen. During the Twenty-first Dynasty when the packets containing the internal organs were returned to the empty chest and abdomen, taking up most of the available space, the gaps left were filled with loose sawdust. Such permanent stuffing helped the body to keep its shape and the aromatic resins would have wreathed it in fragrance. During the Late Period (after 600 BC), when embalming was in decline, bodies were often filled completely with molten resin poured through the embalming incision. As Wallis Budge remarked of such mummies, 'Generally speaking, they will last forever.'

After being covered by natron for so long the skin became shrivelled and stiff, so to restore its suppleness the whole body was rubbed with more than one application of a sweet-smelling lotion of juniper oil, beeswax, natron, spices, milk and wine. The 'Ritual of Embalming' makes it clear that this massaging took place before the embalming incision had been closed: 'Beware lest he be turned upside down onto his abdomen or his face, for his body is filled with medicinal materials and the gods which are within his abdomen might be displaced from their positions.' In other words, care had to be taken while the body was moved during its anointing in case the Canopic packages and their attendant figurines of the Sons of Horus inadvertently fell out through the embalming incision. It was probably just afterwards that the lips of the wound were drawn together and covered with a plate of gold foil or wax bearing the *wedjat*-eye and held in position by molten resin. The *wedjat*, representing the eye of the falcon god Horus, was a particularly power-

21 *Embalming equipment: wax embalming plate bearing the* wedjat-*eye to protect the embalming incision. Height 8 cm (3 ⅛ in). Wax figures of the Sons of Horus to be wrapped with the internal organs when they were returned to the chest cavity. Height 13.3 cm (5 ³/₁₆). All after 1000 BC. Linen bag containing natron crystals. Deir el-Bahri, Thebes. Eighteenth Dynasty, c.1450 BC.*

22 *Head of the unwrapped mummy of the Theban priestess Henttawy showing the results of overstuffing by the embalmers during cosmetic treatment. This mummy has been restored recently to show she would have appeared before her cheeks split. Twenty-first Dynasty, c.1040 BC. (Cairo Museum.)*

23 *Gold leaf eyes and tongues placed over the eye-sockets and within the mouths of mummies of the Graeco–Roman Period. After 305 BC. Length of largest eye 2.9 cm (1 1/6 in); length of largest tongue 5 cm (1 15/16 in).*

ful symbol to avert evil from the entrance into the corpse and to help magically heal the wound. The edges beneath were rarely sewn up, but when they were the stitches were large and untidy resembling nothing so much as those seen on Frankenstein's monster.

Although the anointing restored the skin's suppleness, it still hung in loose folds where the flesh beneath had been dissolved. On the other hand, the arms and legs were emaciated and the features of the face pinched and shrunken. During the Twenty-first Dynasty, therefore, it became the practice to pack linen pads under the skin, or even mud and sawdust, inserted through freshly-made incisions in an effort to restore some lifelike plumpness. Occasionally, though, the stuffing was over-done: the mummy of the Theban priestess Henttawy was not properly dried when her shrunken cheeks were rather fully packed; as the flesh of the face dried out the skin grew tighter over the wads of linen beneath and eventually cracked under the strain. Henttawy's mummy is current-ly exhibited in Cairo Museum with her beauty restored through judi-cious removal of the extra packing and restitching.

The empty cranium was probably dealt with earlier just after the brain was extracted, but now, in addition, the nostrils, ears and mouth were usually plugged with linen or, in some instances, wax. Sometimes, too, a tongue-shaped piece of gold leaf was placed over the actual tongue. But nothing could be done to restore the eyes, so they were pushed down into the sockets and covered with resinated pads of linen over which the eyelids were drawn. In the case of Ramesses III eyes were painted in black on the pads, but it was not until the introduction of artificial eyes with obsidian pupils and alabaster whites that a startlingly lifelike glance was given to certain mummies. One curious custom was the placing of onion skins or even whole bulbs over the eyes or stuffing them into the ears or the body cavity. Their significance is uncertain but may be con-nected with the rituals of the Festival of Sokaris, a Memphite funerary god, during which onions were worn and sniffed. Perhaps they were placed on the mummy to stimulate the breathing of the deceased.

Finally, the whole body was coated with molten resin to toughen it and render it waterproof. But before the bandaging began the last cos-metic touches were applied. The soles of the feet and palms of the hands might be stained with henna; during the Graeco-Roman Period (after 305 BC), many mummies had gold leaf applied to the face, chest and nails. For women the cheeks would be rouged, the lips stained and the eyebrows painted. Sometimes an elaborate wig of human hair with carefully curled ringlets was placed on the head. Some mummies were dressed in sandals, shirts, shifts and other articles of daily dress. Often the whole body was painted, with red ochre in the case of male mummies, yellow for females. The same colouring convention was observed for the sexes in painted statues, coloured reliefs and wall-paintings until the mid-Eighteenth Dynasty. The idea behind it was that, even if he were the highest official in the land, it was the man of the house who went out in the sun and got a tanned skin. On the other hand, no highly-born woman would allow herself to be seen except with a pale skin; if she had to go out into strong sunshine she was suitably covered or carried a sun-shade. The only

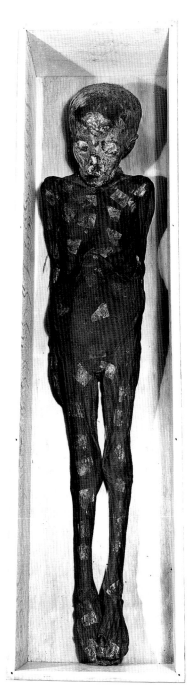

24 *Unwrapped mummy of a very young child with gilded rectangles decorating the face and body. Roman Period, after 30 BC. Length 1.11 m (3 ft 8 in).*

25 *Mummy of a youth outwardly elaborately wrapped in bandages arranged in intricate geometric patterns with a portrait panel inserted over the face. Inside, the body itself was in an advanced state of decomposition before treatment and the bones are in jumbled confusion. Hawara. Roman Period, early second century AD. Length 1.32 m (4 ft 4 1/4 in).*

women with sun-tanned skins would be those who belonged to the lowest social class, such as field workers.

The bodies of the wealthiest clients would also be bedecked with jewellery before the bandaging began. Tutankhamun had six bracelets crowded onto one forearm and seven on the other. But that total was easily surpassed by King Psusennes of the Twenty-first Dynasty whose mummy was found at Tanis; no less than twenty-two bangles were placed on his arms, and he also wore twenty-seven rings on his fingers and thumbs. Even non-royal mummies which managed to escape the attentions of tomb robbers have been discovered wearing the diadems, girdles, finger-rings, collars, necklaces and pectorals which they had once worn in life.

Some fifteen days were allotted to the bandaging of the mummy. It took so long because every action was carefully prescribed and had to be accompanied by the appropriate magical utterances and gestures. Great care was generally expended on the wrapping because the tightness of the bandaging would help to maintain the shape and rigidity of the body. Indeed, by the Graeco-Roman Period all the care was taken on the wrapping whereas the body itself was quite often poorly embalmed: some mummies of this period are just a jumble of bones within a stiffened shell of wrappings formed from bandages arranged into intricate geometrical patterns. The linen used often consisted of worn-out domestic articles such as household towels and cloths or discarded clothing, which explains the reference in a funeral lament to the 'cast-off linen of yesterday' in which the dead now sleeps. Wealthier and more fortunate clients were wrapped in bandages made from the cast-off garments of divine statues. Daily temple ritual required that the cult statue of the temple god, kept hidden in a shrine in the holy of holies, should be dressed each day in best quality linen. When the garments were disposed of because they had become worn and so quite unsuitable for the divine statue, it seems that they could be acquired to provide sanctified mummy wrappings. The rest of the linen, to judge from its markings, was bought especially for the occasion from textile shops. Because it came from such varied sources the linen used to wrap the mummy ranged widely in quality from gossamer-thin gauze of the finest texture to coarse, canvas-like cloth.

Before the wrapping began, all the linen to be used was grouped together in piles according to size and purpose and the top piece in each pile was appropriately marked. In one pile would be shrouds, usually seven in number for magical reasons. In others would be padding, whether specially prepared and shaped wadding or just folded material. Finally, there would be roll upon roll of bandages, the longest up to 15 m (49 ft) in length and anything up to 20 cm (8 in) wide. It has been calculated that a single mummy might be wrapped in up to 375 square m (448 1/2 square yards) of material, so every inch of the workshop floor must have been stacked with linen.

First, the mummy was swathed in a shroud stained saffron yellow. The actual bandaging began with the toes and fingers which were individually wrapped in strips of the finest quality linen; it was at this stage that Tutankhamun and King Psusennes had precious metal stalls fitted over their toe- and finger-nails before the whole of the hands and feet were wrapped. Then a long strip of linen, starting from the right shoulder, was carefully passed around the head, criss-crossing in a figure-of-eight pattern. Sometimes, too, a kind of chin strap was passed under the chin and knotted on top of the head. Next the arms, beginning from the hands and working towards the shoulders, were wrapped before being bound in with the torso. Finally, the wrapping continued down from the head along the legs to the feet until all the limbs had been bandaged in with the rest of the body. Throughout the bandaging process each layer was painted with molten resin to make the wrappings stick together and improve their rigidity. In addition, shaped rolls and folded wads of linen were placed in every nook and cranny, especially on the head, to help give a solid outline to the finished article. Some unfortunate mummies, of course, for one reason or another no longer had the requisite limbs or appendages, and for them so-called 'embalmers' restorations' were provided: artificial hands and feet, arms and legs, even genital organs, usually formed from rolled up and moulded linen, sometimes stiffened with resin and often looking quite realistic, were placed within the wrappings where the real limbs should have been.

Although there were always exceptions, non-royal mummies for the most part had their arms stretched out along the torso. Women usually had their hands extended on the inner or outer thighs; men usually had them spread out modestly over the genital organs. Apart from the earliest part of the Middle Kingdom it was virtually only during the Ptolemaic Period (305–30 BC) that the arms of male mummies were crossed over the chest. For the mummies of pharaohs, however, from the early Eighteenth Dynasty this pose came to be standard.

The wrapping was completed when one or more shrouds, usually dyed red, completely enveloped the mummy, held in place by one or more long bandages running the length of the body and other shorter ones running diagonally from the shoulders and around the body at intervals On average a shroud was more than 4.5 m (14 ½ ft) in length and 1.2 m (4 ft) in width, rather larger than might be expected, as it had to be of sufficient dimensions to be knotted at top and bottom behind the head and feet of the mummy. As many as twenty layers of alternating shrouds and bandages have been counted on some bodies; others are so well wrapped up as to be quite cylindrical in outline. Yet a few mummies of Roman date are tightly bound in only a few layers so that the features are clearly visible through the bandages and are picked out in paint, as in the earliest mummies of the Old Kingdom.

During the Twenty-first and Twenty-second Dynasties mummies often wore, on top of their bandages or just below the surface, red leather straps which lay over the shoulders and were crossed at the front, and sometimes at the back too; they look for all the world like braces except that they support nothing. At the point of intersection additional

26 *Well-wrapped mummy of a young woman found in the coffin of the Theban priest Pasheryenhor. Twenty-second to Twenty-sixth Dynasties, c. 950–650 BC. Length 1.55 m (5 ft 1 in).*

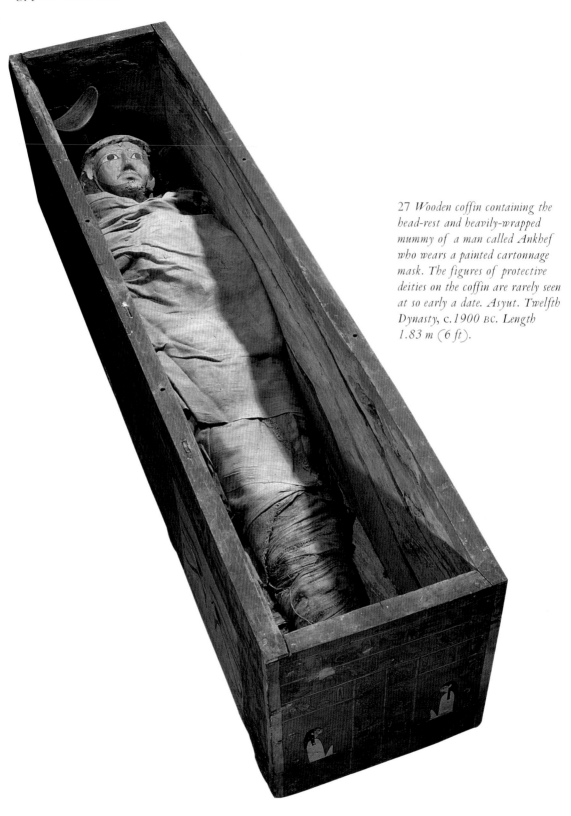

27 *Wooden coffin containing the head-rest and heavily-wrapped mummy of a man called Ankhef who wears a painted cartonnage mask. The figures of protective deities on the coffin are rarely seen at so early a date. Asyut. Twelfth Dynasty, c.1900 BC. Length 1.83 m (6 ft).*

strips of leather were often inserted, one end shaped like a tassel, the other like the counterpoise of a collar bearing the name of the king or High Priest of Amun at the time when the braces were manufactured. The purpose of these mummy braces is quite unknown. For an equally unknown reason, from the Twenty-fifth Dynasty until the Roman Period, many mummies had an outer covering of a network of blue glazed composition beads or even a complete multi-coloured beadwork shroud which almost looks knitted. Poorer clients had an imitation net painted on the outermost layer of their bandages. Some mummies wore an actual net made of knotted string.

It was generally last of all that the mummy mask was fitted over the head and shoulders. Already during the troubled First Intermediate Period (about 2100 BC) the bodies of local noblemen wore masks of linen stiffened with plaster – a material called 'cartonnage'- which represented the face of the deceased framed by a long wig, usually with a broad collar beneath which lay over the chest. Although the features are rarely a true portrait, the mask clearly served to identify the wrapped mummy underneath, presumably for the benefit of the Ka and Ba when they returned to the burial chamber. Often the face was gilded, but for royalty the mask must usually have been completely of gold, to judge from

28 Above top Body of a man, unusually well-embalmed for the period, tightly wrapped in a few layers of bandages with details picked out in paint, a style reminiscent of the earliest mummies of the Old Kingdom. Roman Period, after 30 BC. Length 1.62 m (5 ft 4 in).

29 Above bottom Mummy of a Palace official called Ameniryirt covered with a network of blue beads into which have been incorporated glazed composition figures of the Sons of Horus and a winged funerary scarab. Twenty-fifth Dynasty, c.725 BC. Length 1.67 m (5 ft 5 3/4 in).

30 *Gilded cartonnage mummy mask wearing a vulture headdress, now identified as a noblewoman called Sat-Djehuty. Early Eighteenth Dynasty, c.1500 BC. Height 61 cm (2 ft).*

the most famous example of all, on the mummy of Tutankhamun, and another worn by King Psusennes, buried at Tanis some four hundred years later. For another thousand years mummy masks continued to be an essential part of the funerary equipment, but by the end they were obviously mass-produced and lack the individuality of some of the earlier examples. Yet as the workmanship deteriorated, so, in an attempt to disguise the fact, an ever greater use was made of gilding. Recently, masks of the Graeco-Roman Period (after 305 BC) have aroused great interest, not because of their dubious artistic merit, but because of the cartonnage from which they are made. In some instances, instead of being formed from linen stiffened with plaster, old sheets of written papyrus were used. Now that a technique has been developed by which the papyrus can be extracted without damaging the outward appearance of the mask, many interesting texts, written in Egyptian as well as Greek, are coming to light.

During the Roman Period (after 30 BC), many of the Greeks who had settled in Egypt adopted native burial customs including embalming but at the same time introduced to these ancient practices some new elements which had their origins in the Hellenistic world rather than in the Egyptian. Instead of an Egyptian-style mask, Greek mummies, especially those buried in the cemeteries of Middle Egypt, usually wore a hollow plaster head with realistically modelled features and vividly painted details. An even more lifelike appearance was achieved from the second century AD onwards when the eyes were made from glass rather than just being painted. At first the plaster mould fitted exactly over the wrapped mummy's head and was tied in place through holes in its base. Gradually, though, it came to be raised at an angle to the body, creating the illusion that the deceased was reclining against a rather high pillow.

At the same time as these portrait heads were in use, from the middle of the first century AD it became the custom to insert within the mummy wrappings over the face area a wooden panel on which a most naturalistic portrait of the deceased had been painted. Because the first examples were found on bodies buried in the cemeteries of Greek settlements in the Faiyum, they are usually called 'Faiyumic portraits', although they have been found elsewhere

31 *Gilded cartonnage mummy mask with typically idealised features. There are funerary scenes and a garbled text at the back. Graeco-Roman Period, late first century BC to early first century AD. Height 44 cm (17 5/16 in).*

subsequently. The portrait was usually executed in coloured wax by a technique known as 'encaustic painting'. Watercolours were used less often, probably because they were more liable to damage by air and moisture. First, the features were outlined on the wood, then the background, hair, jewellery and drapery were filled in with liquid wax in which colour had been mixed, applied with a brush. Areas of flesh received a particularly thick layer. The finished portrait depicted the head and shoulders of the deceased, turned slightly to one side and wearing everyday costume. The best examples are so lifelike that the dead themselves might almost be looking out from the bandages as though through the glass panel of a coffin. The use of portrait masks and panels continued until the early fourth century AD when the rise of Christianity in Egypt caused mummification to be abandoned.

The few surviving tomb scenes concerned with the embalming process all deal with the latest stages of the wrapping because the mummy is always shown already wearing its mask. The body lies supported at foot and neck on blocks while two embalmers adjust the bandages or paint them with molten resin which is kept heated in a cauldron over a brazier and applied with brushes. In one scene too damaged to be interpreted, the cauldron and brazier have been replaced by wooden chests; in another, eleven pottery saucers standing on the floor of the embalming workshop probably contain oils and unguents for the final anointings. In a third, a man with engraving tools applies finishing touches. In all these scenes the activities are supervised by a scribe or Lector Priest who stands with rolled papyrus, his hand raised in a ritual gesture while reciting appropriate instructions or spells.

During the Graeco-Roman Period (after 305 BC) in order to identify a body while it was in the embalmer's workshop or being transported (apparently a constant stream of mummies was being shipped around Egypt from the place of death to that of burial) a tablet, usually wooden, was tied around its neck giving the name of the deceased in Egyptian or Greek or both. Quite often these mummy labels also gave the names

32 Early and realistically modelled painted plaster head-covering from a Roman mummy. Diospolis parva. Early first century AD. Height 25.4 cm (10 in).

33 *Wooden mummy labels. Above: beneath a scene of the mummy in its vaulted coffin is a prayer in demotic for a Theban priest called Nespameter. Ptolemaic Period, first century* BC. *Height 12.5 cm (4 ¹¹/₁₂ in). Below: a Greek text names Apollos who died aged fifty. Roman Period, second to fourth centuries* AD. *Width 17.9 cm (7 ¹/₁₆ in).*

of the dead person's parents, his profession, age, even the date of death and the place where the body was to be buried. Indeed, the demotic text was couched in the form of a short prayer that the soul of the deceased might serve and follow Osiris in the Underworld so the label could have been used by penny-pinching relatives as a cheap substitute for a stone burial stela.

Chapter Three | Jewellery and Amulets

At every stage of the wrapping funerary jewellery and amulets were placed on the body within the bandages at specified positions. Jewellery intended solely for the use of the dead can usually be distinguished quite easily from that worn by the living and taken to the tomb with them when they died: funerary jewellery is just too flimsy to have survived normal wear but would have suffered no damage on an immobile mummy. The material preferred for beads is easily-broken glazed composition rather than stone; gilded plaster or wood masquerades as precious metal, or when real gold is used it is wafer-thin and very fragile. Funerary collars frequently have no holes pierced through their terminals, so can never have had fastening threads, and often lack the counterpoise which was worn between the shoulder blades to counterbalance the weight of the collar lying over the chest – or if there is a counterpoise it is too light to serve its purpose. Such collars can never have been worn in life; they could only have been laid on the mummy and held in place by its wrappings.

The wearing of funerary jewellery conferred special protection upon the mummy. Tutankhamun wore a magnificent flexible gold collar inlaid with coloured glass in the form of a vulture with outstretched wings in accordance with Chapter 157 of the *Book of the Dead*, entitled 'Spell for the vulture of gold placed at the throat of the deceased'. The text makes it clear that the vulture was thought of as representing the goddess Isis and as she kept safe her own son Horus within her encircling wings so she would keep safe the mummy. It ends with the words: 'to be spoken over a vulture of gold inscribed with this spell and given as a magical protection to the deceased on the day of burial', and adds, 'a truly excellent spell, proved a million times'.

The papyri on which the text of the *Book of the Dead* was written also contain small paintings or drawings called vignettes which accompany most of the chapters or spells and illustrate their contents. So, although the text of Chapter 158 only required that the mummy wear a broad collar of gold, the accompanying vignette shows that the collar was to have its terminals in the shape of falcons' heads. Tutankhamun wore just such a collar on his mummy, made of very thin sheet gold with engraved details. Another, formed this time from strings of beads, is represented as being worn on his mummy mask. Six hundred years earlier the same kind of collar was illustrated among the rows of possessions depicted inside wooden coffins of Middle Kingdom date (about 2000 BC) and intended to replace by magical means the actual grave goods of the deceased, should they be destroyed or stolen. These illustrations and surviving collars, like that on Tutankhamun's mummy, reveal something which the *Book of the Dead* vignette did not: the counterpoise of the falcon collar was also in the shape of a falcon's head. Since the wearing of this collar granted the dead the protection of the great gods of Heliopolis it became an essential piece of funerary jewellery. During the

34 Opposite *Chapters 156, 159–60, 155, 158, 157 and 154 of the* Book of the Dead *in a hieratic funerary papyrus illustrated by vignettes showing respectively* tit, wadj *and* djed *amulets, falcon and vulture collars and the mummy, warmed by the sun, lying on a bier with bags of natron (?) beneath. Ptolemaic Period, c.300 BC. Height 31 cm (12 3/16).*

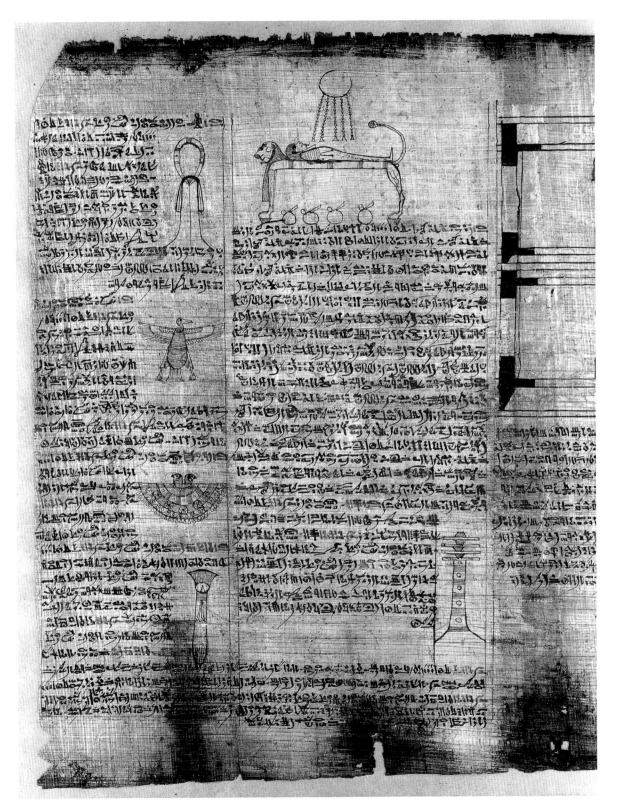

35 *Detail of the inside decoration of the wooden outer coffin of the physician Seni showing a painted frieze of falcon collars with their falcon-headed counterpoises. El-Bersha. Twelfth Dynasty, c.1900 BC. Height 15 cm (5 ⁷/₈ in).*

second century AD, more than twenty-two centuries after it was first depicted inside Middle Kingdom coffins, foreign settlers in Egypt still chose to have it picked out in gold leaf on the outside of their coffins.

A very rare piece of funerary jewellery found on the mummy of Tutankhamun was the Two Ladies collar, again made from thin sheet gold with engraved details. At its centre, side by side and flanked by falcons' wings, were the bodies of the vulture goddess Nekhbet and the cobra goddess Wadjit. Almost from the beginning of Egyptian history these goddesses, who represented symbolically the kingdoms of Upper and Lower Egypt, gave special protection to the person of Pharaoh himself, and so a collar in their form would most fittingly be found on a king's mummy. Yet in Middle Kingdom coffins it was also depicted along with other pieces of essentially royal equipment among the possessions of the non-royal dead. The Middle Kingdom (about 2040–1786 BC) was a time when funerary beliefs and practices were democratised. Previously, the right to be embalmed and the prospect of a guaranteed afterlife were restricted to royalty and great noblemen; now the opportunity was open to all (as long as they could afford it!). Funerary texts which had been composed solely to aid the dead king to reach heaven and had been inscribed inside pyramids were now copied by commoners inside their wooden coffins. Everything was taken over lock, stock and barrel with

little thought for the appropriateness. Thus possessions like the Two Ladies collar, crowns and other royal insignia which should only belong to a king were depicted inside the coffins of commoners who really had no use for them in this world or the next.

In addition to funerary jewellery, amulets of every form and material were placed among the layers of mummy wrappings in considerable numbers. Often several hundred have been found on a single body. Strictly speaking, the type of amulet and its position on the body were laid down in some detail in the various funerary texts, but sometimes the impression given is that the embalmer just grabbed a handful of amulets and scattered them among the bandages. As in the case of funerary jewellery the provision of some amulets was required by certain chapters of the *Book of the Dead*.

One amulet found on almost every mummy and made from materials as varied as precious metal, stone, glazed composition, glass and wood was the curiously shaped *djed*-pillar with its distinctive four short crossbars at the top. One suggestion is that originally it represented a stylised tree trunk with its branches lopped off. Certainly, when it first appears, in connection with the rites for Sokaris, the funerary god of Memphis, and later for Ptah, a more powerful god of the same area, it was the central feature of the ceremony known as 'The Raising of the *Djed*'. Since

36 *Vignettes from the* Book of the Dead *of the scribe Any showing* djed, tit, ib *and* weres *amulets to illustrate chapters 155,156, 29B and 166. Nineteenth Dynasty, c.1250 BC. Height 5.5 cm (2 1/6 in).

this entailed setting upright a large *djed* by means of ropes, rather in the manner of a maypole, the tree trunk origin seems highly likely. Later, however, Osiris, god of the dead, adopted the *djed* as one of his symbols and from that time onwards it was looked upon as a stylised representation of the god's backbone. At any rate, Chapter 155 of the *Book of the Dead* concerns only Osiris and the backbone connection. The spell is entitled 'Words to be spoken over a *djed*-pillar of gold, strung upon a fibre of sycamore . . . and placed at the throat of the deceased on the day of burial'. The text addresses the god: 'Raise yourself up, Osiris! You have your backbone once more, O weary-hearted one; you have your vertebrae.' So the placing of a *djed*-pillar on a mummy granted the deceased stability.

Also connected with the Osiris legend was Chapter 156, a spell to be spoken over a *tit*-amulet of red jasper, the colour of the blood of the goddess Isis. In fact, any red or even green material seems to have been sufficient! This amulet was thought to represent the knotted girdle of the goddess and accordingly, if placed at the throat of the deceased, the power of Isis would be 'the magical protection of his limbs'. Chapters 159 and 160 were to be pronounced over a papyrus-shaped amulet of green felspar called a *wadj*. As the papyrus was green, full of sap and the promise of new life, the placing of the *wadj*-amulet on the mummy would grant the deceased eternal rejuvenation.

The vignette of Chapter 166 shows an amulet shaped like a head-rest of the type which Egyptians used instead of a pillow when they slept. Although the basic shape was always a curved support for the neck set on top of a pillar, which nearly always looks too high for comfort to Western eyes, the pillar might take a variety of shapes. Tutankhamun had a full-sized ivory headrest in the form of Shu, god of air, supporting the curved neck-rest on his shoulders in the same way as he was thought to support the heavens. Flanking him were two recumbent lions facing outwards, the lions of the horizon over whose backs the sun rose every day. Possession of a head-rest amulet (called a *weres*) meant that the head of the deceased would be eternally raised up, just as the sun rose eternally. The text of Chapter 166 promises further that the head of the deceased will never be taken away, a fate which seems to have been a constant worry. The usual material for the head-rest amulet was an iron ore called haematite, but Tutankhamun had one wrapped behind his head which was made from pure iron, a very rare occurrence of this metal in Egypt for the time.

The Egyptians held the heart to be of the utmost importance, for they considered it the seat of the intelligence and all emotions. Consequently, no less than four spells in the *Book of the Dead* were concerned with preventing its removal from the body or ensuring its quick return. Curiously enough, considering that the Egyptians had first hand knowledge of the heart because of the embalming process, during which it was often inadvertently removed, the heart-shaped amulet (called an *ib*) looks more like an elongated globular pot with two handles and a high rim. Chapter 26 was to be inscribed on a heart of lapis lazuli, Chapter 27 on one of feldspar and Chapter 29 on one of green stone, possibly serpentine. Chapter 28 had no specific instructions about the material.

Most important of all the spells concerned with the heart was Chapter 30B of the *Book of the Dead* which was always to be inscribed 'on a scarab made from green stone [probably jasper], mounted in fine gold, with a silver suspension ring and placed at the throat of the deceased'. The spell was reputed to be very old, having been found in Hermopolis, under the feet of the majesty of this god (that is, beneath a statue of the god Thoth). It was written on a block of Upper Egyptian mineral in the writing of the god himself and was discovered in the time of the majesty of the King of Upper and Lower Egypt, Menkaure, justified. It was the king's son Hordedef who found it while he was going around making an inspection of the temples.' Menkaure, or Mycerinus as Classical authors called him, was a pharaoh of the Fourth Dynasty who built the smallest of the three pyramids at Giza. Yet the earliest royal heart scarab belonged to King Sobkemsaf II of the Seventeenth Dynasty who reigned about 1590 BC, nine centuries after Mycerinus, and the first firmly dated example was made for a high official of the Thirteenth Dynasty about 1710 BC. Even if heart scarabs were first produced for Middle Kingdom royalty (such an important amulet is unlikely to have been made first for a commoner) but none have survived, it does look suspiciously as though a false pedigree was created for Chapter 30B to make it look older than it really was: the spell was almost certainly only composed a very short time before it was first inscribed on a heart scarab.

To judge from the earliest funerary texts, not even Pharaoh himself expected to enter heaven unopposed; for ordinary mortals entry would always be more difficult. During the Old Kingdom (about 2686–2181 BC) when only the great nobility, apart from the king, were assured of an afterlife, living one's earthly life according to a strict moral code was considered sufficient to secure eternal bliss. But the breakdown of order during the political troubles of the First Intermediate Period which led to tomb robbery and the desecration of cemeteries shattered this belief. So, in an attempt to deter such wrong doing, the idea was encouraged that judgement would be passed on the dead for the actions they had committed upon earth. At first it was an anonymous Great God who

37 *Human-headed green jasper heart scarab set in a gold mount inscribed with a very early version of chapter 30B of the* Book of the Dead. *Tomb robbers, brought to trial c.1109 BC, confessed to stealing it from the mummy of King Sobkemsaf II. Thebes Seventeenth Dynasty, c.1590 BC. Length 3.6 cm (1 ²/₅ in).*

38 Vignette of the Weighing of the Heart of the scribe Any illustrating chapter 125 of his Book of the Dead *papyrus. Nineteenth Dynasty, c.1250 BC. Height 38 cm (15 in).*

passed sentence, but once Osiris became supreme god of the dead during the Middle Kingdom, it was only natural that he should be the god before whom the trial took place.

To find out whether the deceased was worthy to enter the Field of Reeds, the Egyptian equivalent of the Elysian Fields, his heart was weighed in a balance. The weighing of the heart, which illustrates Chapter 125, is one of the best-known vignettes in the *Book of the Dead*. The deceased is always shown standing anxiously at one side, often accompanied by his *Ba* and by various forms of his fate or destiny. Jackal-headed Anubis checks that the balance is unbiased; Thoth, ibis-headed scribe of the gods, stands ready to write down the result; and the twelve

great gods usually act as witnesses to the fairness of the trial. A hybrid monster called Ammit (literally 'she who gobbles down' or even 'eater of the dead'), part crocodile, part hippopotamus, part lion (or panther), always lurks nearby, ready to devour any heart found unworthy to enter heaven. The heart itself sits in one of the pans of the balance and is weighed against a figure of the goddess Maat or her symbol, an ostrich feather. Maat was the embodiment of all kinds of abstract concepts such as truth, cosmic order, wisdom, justice and righteousness. Clearly, the idea behind the weighing was that goodness would be rewarded and evil punished, since the wicked heart, heavy with sin, would be unable to balance Maat. Instead, Ammit would seize it for her dinner and the evil dead, deprived of his heart, would be denied an afterlife. However, the text of Chapter 30B addressed the heart in no uncertain words: 'Do not stand against me as witness! Do not oppose me in the tribunal! Do not tilt [the scales] to my disadvantage in the presence of the Guardian of the Balance!' In other words, no matter how wicked the earthly life of the deceased, he could still be sure of heaven if he had a heart scarab inscribed with the relevant spell which would effectively prevent the heart revealing any of his master's sins during the trial. As a result, of course, the heart scarab became virtually the most important funerary amulet known to the Egyptians, and from the early New Kingdom onwards few mummies can have been wrapped without one being placed somewhere within the bandages, preferably near the actual heart.

Scarabs of every material imaginable and quite unconnected with the heart were placed on mummies in numbers. They might be set as the bezels of finger-rings or strung with beads in necklaces or bracelets or just scattered loose among the bandages. After about 900 BC so-called funerary scarabs, always of glazed composition, become common. They are rather large, uninscribed, flanked by separately-made falcon's wings and stitched to the bandages across the mummy's chest or incorporated into a network of beads. The scarab or dung beetle was a symbol of new life or resurrection because the Egyptians mistakenly believed the baby beetles were hatched out as though by spontaneous generation from the ball of dung the adult is seen rolling about.

Only marginally less important than the heart scarab was the *wedjat* which represented the eye of a falcon with its characteristic markings beneath. The falcon-headed god to whom the eye was thought to belong originally was Horus the Elder, called by the Greeks Haroeris, an early creation god whose right eye was the sun, his left the moon. It was believed that during the never-ending struggle between Horus, who protected the fertile Nile valley, and his eternal enemy Seth, god of the arid desert, the left eye was plucked out but was healed and restored to its rightful owner by Thoth – *wedjat* actually means 'that which is whole or sound'. Perhaps it was the regular waning and waxing of the moon which suggested the whole idea that the left lunar eye was 'damaged' and 'healed'. Interestingly, in Egyptian mathematics the various parts of the *wedjat* were each given a fractional value and when all the parts were added together they amounted to sixty-three sixty-fourths;

39 Male mummy wearing a frame strung with tiny gilded wooden amulets. Painted on the outer shroud secured by cross-straps is a full-length representation of Osiris wearing a red garment with a star pattern. Roman Period, after 30 BC. Height 1.64 m (5 ft 4 3/4 in).

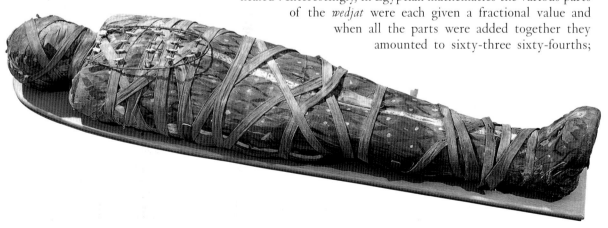

the missing sixty-fourth was presumably provided magically by Thoth. When Osiris rose to prominence his son, also called Horus but a completely different god from Horus the Elder, assumed greater importance too and actually took over the role of opponent of Seth from his namesake. Consequently, the *wedjat* came to be thought of as the eye of Horus, son of Osiris. Accordingly, in the Osiris legend, Horus offered his healed eye to his dead father and so powerful a charm was it that it brought him back to life! The offering of an *wedjat* would even suffice instead of actual food offerings. The *wedjat*-eye also had great protective powers, which is why it was often depicted on the plate which covered the embalmer's incision. It is not surprising, therefore, that probably more *wedjats* than any other kind of amulet have been found on mummies: there are *wedjats* made of precious metal, glazed composition, stone, glass, even wood or bone, and combinations of these materials. Many represent the right solar eye rather than the left; some are large and elaborately inlaid; others are multiple *wedjats* formed from four or more eyes combined. Chapter 140 of the *Book of the Dead* was a spell 'to complete the lunar *wedjat*'; Chapter 167 was entitled 'to fetch the solar *wedjat*', a reference to the legend in which the solar eye left heaven and had to be brought back.

Small figures of gods and goddesses, no more than a few centimetres in height, were placed among the wrappings to give their special protection to the mummy. The figures might be in the round or in profile, usually made of glazed composition, glass or gilded wood or plaster, but sometimes of solid gold. Deities connected with the Osiris legend were particularly popular: Isis suckling the infant Horus, or a youthful Horus flanked by his mother and her sister Nephthys, or Nephthys kneeling with her hand to her head in the age-old posture of mourning. For the same reason figures of the Four Sons of Horus, of Anubis, often depicted on a plaque as a reclining jackal, and of Thoth carrying the *wedjat* are also common. Amulets in the form of Bes, the ugly little lion-maned spirit who scared away evil demons at the moment of birth, and of the goddess of childbirth herself, the hippopotamus Taweret, were provided because of their association with new life.

Some of the earliest amulets found on mummies represent parts of the body such as hands, legs or faces. It seems they could endow the deceased with their particular bodily functions such as the power of action, movement and use of the senses; they could even act as substitutes should the actual physical parts be destroyed. Perhaps the reason why most of them later came to be no longer considered necessary was that improvements in mummification methods made

40 *Glazed composition amuletic figures: pale green Taweret, hippopotamus goddess of childbirth; light and dark blue Bes, her lion-maned assistant, height 6.9 cm (2 3/4 in); pale green triad of Isis, her son Horus and sister Nephthys, height 3.7 cm (1 1/2 in). All Late Period, after 600 BC.*

41 Above above *Glazed composition amuletic figures of the Four Sons of Horus, the Canopic deities. Late New Kingdom, c.1000 BC. Height of Imsety 14.6 cm (5 ³/₄ in).*

42 Right *Glazed composition amulets. Pectoral plaque depicting Anubis as a reclining jackal with a winged* wedjat-*eye flying above him, New Kingdom, c.1250 BC; winged funerary scarab, pierced for stitching onto a mummy's wrapping, Late Period, after 900 BC, width 14.8 cm (5 ⁵/₆ in); composite amulet formed from* ankh, djed *and* was *signs combined, Gebel Barkal, Twenty-fifth Dynasty, c.700 BC, height 23.1 cm (9 ¹/₁₂ in).*

limbs in particular less likely to become detached or injured. Amulets of animals transferred their particular characteristics to the deceased: the bull or ram conferred virility, the cow, cat or frog fertility. A serpent's head, usually of red material, perhaps ensured cool refreshment to the throat or gave protection from snake bite in the Afterlife. An animal-headed *was*-sceptre granted dominion in the Other World to the deceased. The two fingers amulet, always made of dark-coloured material and placed on the left side of the mummy's pelvis, might represent the two fingers of the embalmer and be intended to reconfirm the mummification process. The staircase amulet represented the stepped dais upon which the throne of Osiris was set or the mound of creation itself; the mason's plummet guaranteed perpetual equilibrium, the carpenter's square eternal rectitude. Curiously enough, one of the best-known amuletic forms, the *ankh* or looped cross, does not occur very often as a funerary amulet. It is thought to represent the tie straps of a sandal or possibly a mirror in its case, and stood for life', 'living', 'alive' and connected ideas, which should have been just what a mummy wanted.

43 *Selection of funerary amulets. Glazed composition hand, length 3.1 cm (1 1/5 in); haematite headrest or* weres, *width 3 cm (1 3/12 in); glazed composition papyrus or* wadj, *length 5.6 cm (2 1/5 in); carnelian snake's head, length 4.4 cm (1 3/4 in); haematite plummet, width at base 1.8 cm (3/4 in); haematite carpenter's square, height 1.5 cm (3/5 in); glazed composition staircase, length 1.9 cm (3/4 in); carnelian leg with foot, height 2.1 cm (13/16 in); glass heart or* ib, *height 5.3 cm (2 1/16 in); obsidian two fingers, height 8.5 cm (3 1/3 in); red jasper Girdle of Isis or* tit, *height 6.5 cm (2 7/12 in). Old Kingdom to Twenty-sixth Dynasty, c.2300–600 BC.*

Chapter Four | Coffins and Sarcophagi

The corpse was now protected physically by embalming and magically by funerary jewellery and dozens of different kinds of amulets placed among its wrappings; even greater protection would be afforded by a coffin or a nest of coffins and an outermost sarcophagus. Strictly speaking, the term sarcophagus should only be applied to a stone coffin, for it comes from the Greek words meaning 'eater of flesh', the name given to a kind of limestone which was actually believed to dissolve any corpse placed within it.

By the late Predynastic Period (just before 3100 BC) some bodies were already being enclosed in small coffins of clay, basketwork or wood instead of being placed directly in the sand. Ironically, it was the introduction of the coffin which led to rapid decomposition of the corpse, for it excluded the very sand which had helped to preserve naturally bodies

44 Early Dynastic skeleton in a reed coffin showing the results of being buried separated from hot, dry sand. Tarkhan, c.3100–3000 BC. Unflexed length 1.58 m (5 ft 2 in).

like 'Ginger'. Basketwork coffins were made from reed stems which were lashed together into short bundles and assembled into sides and floor, while clay coffins were often oval in shape. The earliest wooden coffins of the Archaic Period (Dynasties 1–2) are rather like crates with panelling on the longer sides, short ends extending a little above the level of the longer sides and slightly curved lids. The resemblance to models of contemporary houses is not accidental: throughout Egyptian history a coffin was thought of as a house of eternity for the dead. Whatever the material, all Early Dynastic coffins are almost square in shape because the body within lay tightly wrapped in a hunched-up position on its side. It was not until the Old Kingdom (Dynasties 3–6) that coffins became regularly full-length and rectangular with the introduction of mummification: to provide the embalmer with easy access to the abdomen and internal organs the corpse was stretched out and it was in the same extended position that it was wrapped and buried.

Wooden coffins of the non-royal dead during the Old Kingdom were made from rough planks fastened by dowels, a technique of construction which continued in use until the end of the Middle Kingdom, about a thousand years later. Their decoration was usually quite plain, no more than a horizontal band of hieroglyphs running around all four sides and a single vertical column running down the lid which gave the name and titles of the deceased, and two *wedjat*-eyes painted or carved on one of the longer sides at the head end, through which the mummy inside could look out at the world. Royalty and great noblemen, however, were provided with sarcophagi of granite, basalt, limestone or alabaster. Some had scarcely more decoration than the plainest wooden coffin. Others, like that of King Mycerinus, found inside his pyramid at Giza but lost at sea on its way to England and the British Museum, were elaborately carved with a pattern of recesses called palace façade panelling. This decoration was based on the mud-brick façade of the early Egyptian palace and on some sarcophagi it was also brightly painted in imitation of the coloured fabrics which once hung upon the palace walls. So large and heavy are some of these sarcophagi that they must have been set in place

in the burial chamber before the funeral began, to avoid long delays in the burial ritual while sweating workmen manoeuvred them into position. Indeed, the sarcophagus of King Khufu, which is still within the burial chamber of the Great Pyramid, must have been incorporated into the pyramid while it was still being built, as it is fractionally too large to have been introduced through the internal passages of the tomb.

During the First Intermediate Period the decoration of wooden coffins belonging to local noblemen of Middle Egypt became much more colourful and elaborate. Now, for the first time, representations of the possessions and funerary equipment of the deceased were painted in brightly-coloured detail on the interior surfaces. Spells written in black cursive script in closely crowded vertical columns now make their appearance too. They are known as the 'Coffin Texts' because of their new location, but were based on texts originally inscribed inside the pyramids of the last rulers of the Old Kingdom.

By the early Middle Kingdom, about 2000 BC, the wealthy dead were interred inside an outer and inner rectangular coffin, each made

45 *Wooden inner coffin of the commander Sepi decorated with simple bands of inscription including a prayer for food offerings and, at the head end,* wedjat-*eyes over an elaborately painted False Door. El-Bersha. Twelfth Dynasty, c.1900 BC. Length 2.13 m (6 ft 11 ⁷⁄₈ in).*

from well-cut planks of imported timber joined by dowels, with mitre and tenon joints at the corners and standing on four or more stout battens which ran across the width of the flooring and held it together. The internal walls of both coffins were regularly covered with spells from the Coffin Texts, representations of grave goods and funerary offerings and sometimes a map of the Underworld illustrating the funerary text called *The Book of the Two Ways* which gave the deceased a choice of path to heaven. The outsides of the coffins were often just as elaborately decorated with painted representations of colourful palace façade panelling framed by vertical and horizontal bands of hieroglyphs invoking offerings for the deceased and protection from various gods and goddesses. Even the *wedjat*-eyes, placed so as to be level with the mummy's face, were often incorporated into a painted representation of a False Door so that the dead might not only look out but send his spirit out too.

Poorer burials had to make do with local timber like sycamore or tamarisk, often roughly cut and disguised by a coating of plaster. Their

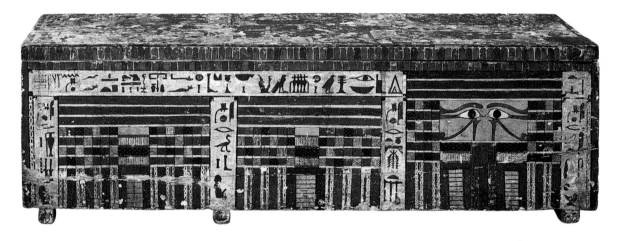

46 Elaborately painted wooden inner coffin with representations of palace façade panelling and wall-hangings, usurped by a man called Amenhotep. Thebes. Twelfth Dynasty, c.1900 BC. Length 2 m (6 ft 6 3/4 in).

only decoration was on the outside walls and comprised the essential *wedjat*-eyes and bands of hieroglyphs containing the name and titles of the deceased and prayers to the gods. Stone sarcophagi are relatively rare in the Middle Kingdom and exclusive to the burials of royalty and great noblemen. Their decoration was usually extremely austere, like that of wooden coffins from poorer burials. But some of the earlier examples, like those belonging to great court ladies who were buried beneath the temple of King Mentuhotep II at Deir el-Bahri in about 2020 BC, are crowded with scenes of the deceased at her toilet, drinking milk fresh from the cow's udders, seated at a banquet or watching butchers at work and grain being stored.

As early as the Eleventh Dynasty the funerary masks on some mummies were extended so that the whole body came to be enveloped in a figure-hugging cover. Because the mummy lay on its left side so that it could look out through the *wedjat*-eyes on its coffin wall, the back of this cover was visible, so it too was modelled to the mummy's contours and decorated. This is how the human-form or anthropoid coffin came into being, made in two parts, back and front – or rather, body and lid. During the Middle Kingdom anthropoid coffins were usually of cartonnage rather than wood, they were without inscription and were still enclosed inside a rectangular outer coffin, but they were to become the most popular shape for coffins for the next two thousand years.

A characteristic variant of the new-fangled anthropoid coffin was developed at Thebes during the late Second Intermediate Period (about 1600 BC). It was always made of wood covered with plaster, massive and roughly formed, being hewn out of a log of local timber in the same way as a dugout canoe but with a lid. The face was framed by a heavy wig with two lappets which extended onto the chest; beneath was a crudely painted broad collar from the lower edge of which ran a single column of hieroglyphs containing an offering formula for the deceased. Because the remainder of the lid was always decorated with a pattern of enveloping protective vultures' wings painted in bright colours, or gilded in the case of royalty, such coffins are known as *rishi* coffins from the Arabic word meaning 'feathered'.

During the course of the Eighteenth Dynasty wooden anthropoid coffins became much less massive, for they were now made of thin planks skilfully dowelled together. At first they were rather plainly decorated with a single band of painted inscription which ran down the length of the lid and was crossed at intervals by transverse bands, the whole arrangement echoing the position of the bandages which held the final shroud in place on the' mummy. The ground colour was white, or even plain unpainted wood, but later a glossy black varnish was used and accordingly the bands of inscription identifying the deceased were painted in yellow or even gilded. Sometimes, of course, the whole coffin was gilded, but only thinly. Quite early on, the panels framed by the bands of inscription were filled by figures of the gods named in the text, namely the Four Sons of Horus, Anubis and Thoth. The goddess Nut always spread her wings protectively over the lid, Nephthys usually knelt at the head end and her sister Isis at the foot. A new feature was that the arms of the deceased were now shown, carved in high relief, usually crossed over the chest and holding amuletic symbols.

By the Ramesside Period (Dynasties 19 and 20) even in quite modest burials the mummy was placed inside a nest of anthropoid wooden coffins, each fitting neatly within the next, right down to an innermost cover or mummy board which lay immediately over the wrapped body. When the funerary mask on the mummy is echoed in

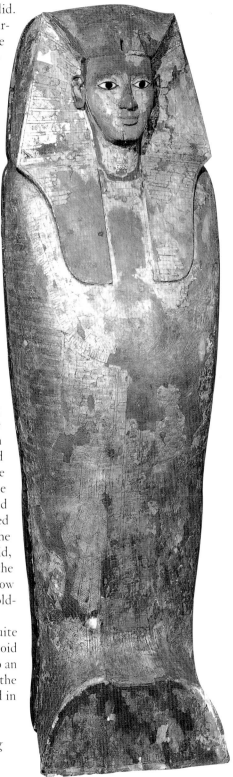

47 Rishi coffin, so-called from its decoration of feathering, made for King Nubkheperre Inyotef from a hollowed-out log overlaid with gilded gesso. Thebes. Seventeenth Dynasty, c.1600 BC. Height 1 7 m (5 ft 6 ¹¹⁄₁₂ in).

48 Right *Gilded wooden inner coffin of the Theban priestess Henutmehit with the bands of inscription following the lines of the outermost bandages on the mummy itself. Nineteenth Dynasty, c.1250 BC. Height 1.88 m (6 ft 2 in).*

49 Far right *Painted wooden inner coffin of the Theban priest Denytenamun wearing the characteristic massive floral collar and red braces crossed over the chest. The superbly carved mask might be a portrait but the vulture head-dress ought more properly to be worn by a woman. Twenty-second Dynasty, c.900 BC. Height 1.88 m (6 ft 2 in).*

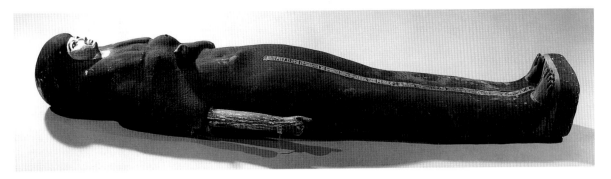

every detail by those on the coffin lids and the remaining decoration on the various lids is identical, the whole effect resembles that of a set of Russian dolls. Sometimes, however, the lid of an inner coffin in female burials shows the deceased not as a mummy but in daily dress, wearing a long, intricately pleated white linen gown, with sandal-clad feet peeping out below the hem and a fashionable wig on her head. Instead of the arms being crossed, one lies across the body just below the breasts (which are realistically modelled) and the other hangs down at her side. To complete the effect of a lady of fashion bangles are worn on her arms, rings on her fingers, studs in her ears and a floral chaplet with central lotus bloom encircles her wig. After the New Kingdom lids showing the deceased in daily dress disappeared but characteristically female wigs continued to be represented on women's coffins and modelled breasts were often depicted, with the nipples patterned to look like flowers.

Throughout this period the decoration of coffins, both inside and out, became more and more crowded with figured panels and amuletic symbols until by the Twenty-first Dynasty (about 1000 BC) every external inch was covered with small, highly-coloured vignettes lightly modelled in plaster before being painted. Most characteristic are the massive many-stranded floral collar which sometimes hangs almost to the thighs, from which separately attached wooden hands often emerge, and the red-painted braces crossed over the chest. From the Twenty-second Dynasty (about 945 BC onwards) it was more usual for innermost coffins to be made of cartonnage rather than wood, closely fitting the contours of the wrapped mummy, laced tightly up the back like an old-fashioned corset and finally sealed with a wooden tablet beneath the feet. Later, a popular scene on the footboard showed the Apis bull, who eventually became linked with Osiris, galloping to the necropolis with a mummy strapped to its back. Now, too, the decoration of both inner and outer coffins was less crowded and hectic, helped by the fact that the figured scenes were much larger and the few inscriptions were usually confined to a single band of hieroglyphs running down the lid or a panel of columns over the lower legs. A constantly recurring decoration on the lid is outspread wings, whether flying on their own, attached to the sky-goddess Nut or a scarab, or outstretched, one up and one down, and appended to a snake or a goddess as often as to a bird.

The repertoire of scenes which could be drawn upon to decorate the outer surfaces of coffins was enormous. Anubis tending the wrapped

50 *Painted cartonnage coffin with gilded face made for the Theban priestess Tjaiastenimu although containing the mummy of a child. Under the resin coating the owner appears to wear daily dress. The positioning of the wooden attached arms is not common. Twenty-second Dynasty, c.900 BC. Length 1.51 m (4 ft 11 1/2 in).*

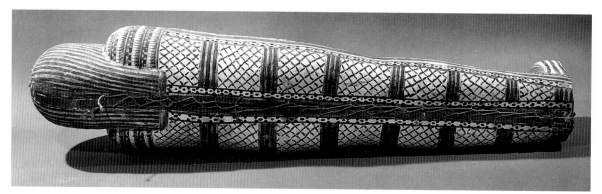

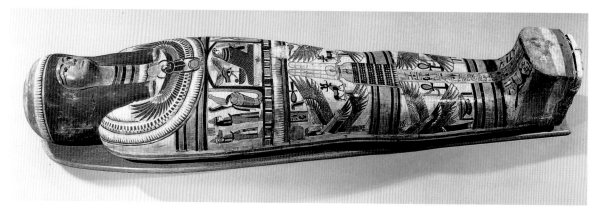

mummy, the funeral procession and the final rites at the tomb, the weighing of the heart, tree-goddesses dispensing water to thirsty *Bas*; the Hathor cow emerging from the western mountain, which marked the land of the dead; the sun-god's boat being drawn through the Underworld; the world's creation symbolised by the separation of Geb from Nut; and the adoration of various funerary gods and symbols and Underworld inhabitants all occur on one coffin or another. Popular themes for the decoration of internal surfaces were representations of the deified King Amenophis I, or simply his name in a cartouche; Osiris or his emblem the *djed*-pillar painted on a large scale; an equally gigantic figure of the goddess of the West or of Nut; scenes of purification, offering and adoration; the presentation of the deceased to various gods; and

51 Opposite, top *Painted cartonnage inner coffin of the Theban priestess Tjentmutengebtyu. The gilded face and vulture head-dress are a sign of her rank. Twenty-second Dynasty, c.900 BC. Height 1.69 m (5 ft 6 in).*

52 Opposite, centre above *Painted cartonnage inner coffin of the man Djedameniufankh with an unusual predominantly blue ground. Twenty-second Dynasty, c.800 BC. Height 1.81 m (5 ft 11 1/4 in).*

53 Opposite, centre below *Laced-up back of the cartonnage inner coffin of Djedameniufankh. The lozenge patterning presumably imitates a beadwork netting on the actual mummy. Twenty-second Dynasty, c.800 BC. Height 1.81 m (5 ft 11 1/4 in).*

54 Opposite below *Carefully painted cartonnage inner coffin of the Theban priest Nespernub. The motif of wings and the restriction of the text to a single column over the lower legs are characteristic. Twenty-second Dynasty, c.800 BC. Height 1.73 m (5 ft 8 in).*

55 *The Apis bull carrying the mummy to the tomb as depicted on the wooden footboard of the painted cartonnage inner coffin of the Theban priest Hor. Deir el-Bahri, Thebes. Twenty-fifth Dynasty, c.700 BC. Width 21 cm (8 1/4 in).*

56 *Painted wooden inner coffin of the Libyan Pasenhor covered with texts and scenes including the weighing of the deceased's heart. The Osiris emblem at the neck is very unusual. Thebes. Twenty-fifth Dynasty, c.700 BC. Height 2.03 m (6 ft 8 in).*

57 *Highly decorated interior of the wooden coffin of the Theban priest Amenemipt. Below the cartouche of the deified King Amenophis I, the deceased and his Ba adore or make offering to various deities. In one scene his mummy is purified while at the sides are rows of animal-headed mummiform gods. Twenty-first to Twenty-second Dynasty, c.950–900 BC. Height 2.10 m (6 ft 10 ³/4 in).*

row after row of monstrous Underworld beings with mummiform bodies and nightmare heads. Any square inch of space left was filled with amuletic signs. Because the outsides of coffins were coated with a thick yellow varnish their colours are often rather dulled but the inside surfaces usually retain their original technicolour brilliance.

Royalty and great noblemen throughout the New Kingdom were interred within an outermost stone sarcophagus. In non-royal burials sarcophagi were anthropoid as early as the mid-Eighteenth Dynasty (about 1400 BC) and during the Ramesside Period sometimes depicted the deceased in daily dress, but for royalty at first they were rectangular, carved with figures of funerary deities framed by bands of religious text. Sometimes the head-end was rounded to give a cartouche-shape in outline and from the early Nineteenth Dynasty a figure of the king was often sculpted in high relief on the lid. All the inner and outer surfaces came to be covered with small scenes and inscriptions culled from popular funerary texts such as *The Book of Gates* or *The Book of What is in the Underworld*, and a gigantic figure of the sky-goddess Nut dominated the interior. Tomb robbers have left enough evidence to suggest that the inner anthropoid coffins were usually of gilded wood but to judge from tomb-equipment of Tutankhamun and the rulers buried at Tanis, one at least of them might have been of solid precious metal.

When the New Kingdom ended stone sarcophagi fell out of use for nearly three hundred years before regaining their popularity in the Late Period, after about 650 BC. Then, for royalty, the outermost coffin was a massive rectangular hard-stone box with curved head-end and a figure of the deceased sculpted on the lid, while every surface inside and out was covered with scenes and texts from funerary books. Wealthy commoners, too, had stone outer coffins identical in shape and decoration with those of royalty, but the lid was mummiform and depicted the deceased wearing a divine beard and a large collar, and sometimes carrying amulets, although usually the hands were never shown.

Most burials, however, still employed wooden outer coffins which were nearly always anthropoid although from the Twenty-fifth Dynasty

58 *Black granite sarcophagus of the Viceroy of Nubia Merymose, one of the earliest mummiform stone coffins made for a commoner. Eighteenth Dynasty, c.1380 BC. Length 1.98 m (6 ft 6 in).*

a rectangular form with protruding posts at each corner and a vaulted lid occurs. Indeed, during the Roman Period (after 30 BC) such a coffin was often the only one in a burial, crudely painted with mythological scenes and dominated inside by a huge figure of Nut. A full-length portrait of the deceased in daily dress painted on the outermost shroud covering the mummy sometimes had to suffice instead of a proper inner coffin. Cartonnage inner coffins actually did continue until the end of the Ptolemaic Period but by then they were often made up of separate sections covering the head and shoulders, chest, legs and feet, all brightly painted and smothered with gilding.

Usually, however, throughout the Late Dynastic Period (after 664 BC) anthropoid coffins were of wood, inner ones at first being distinguished by representing the deceased standing on an often quite high platform, hence the term 'pedestal' type. They might be plain and unvarnished with text confined to the centre of the lid but more often all surfaces, front and back, inside and out, were a sea of hieroglyphs among which the few small figured scenes on the lid were all but swamped. There was always at least one pair of outspread wings some-

59 Outer wooden and inner cartonnage coffins of the Theban priest Hor. The shape of the outer coffin with protruding posts at each corner and vaulted lid is characteristic of the period. Deir el-Bahri, Thebes. Twenty-fifth Dynasty, c.700 BC. Length 2.15 m (7 ft ½ in).

60 *Inside of the vaulted lid of the wooden coffin of the Theban governor Soter, showing the sky-goddess Nut flanked by zodiac signs and the twenty-four hours personified. Abd el-Qurna, Thebes. Roman Period, early second century* AD. *Length 2.13 m (7 ft).*

63 Opposite, left *Inner wooden coffin of the lady Seshepenmehit. The green colour of the face links the deceased with Osiris as vegetation god. Thebes. Twenty-sixth Dynasty, c.650 BC. Height 1.71 m (5 ft 7 1/4 in).*

64 Opposite, right *Floor of the outer wooden coffin of the lady Seshepenmehit decorated with a huge figure of falcon-headed Osiris-Sokaris, a funerary god. Thebes. Twenty-sixth Dynasty, c.650 BC. Height 2.03 m (6 ft 8 in).*

61 Right *Wooden coffin, the lid adorned with a snake, containing the mummy of a Roman child wrapped in a shroud on which is painted a full-length portrait of the deceased in daily dress. Third century AD. Length 95.5 cm (3ft 1 3/8 in).*

62 Below *Wooden inner coffin and mummy of Djedhor wearing separate cartonnage mask, breast, thigh and feet covers. The use of blue pigment is very rare, the bright paint and gilding characteristic. Akhmim. Thirtieth Dynasty, c.350 BC. Length of coffin 1.76 m (5 ft 9 1/4 in); length of mummy 1.56 m (5 ft 1 1/2 in).*

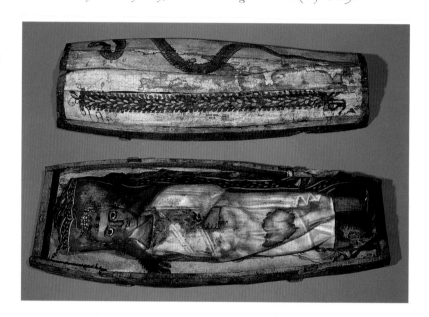

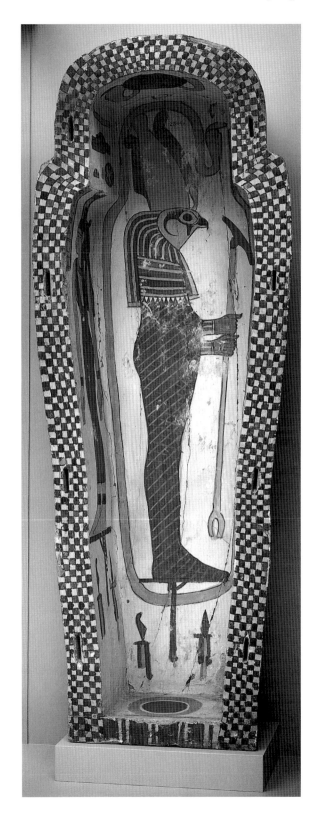

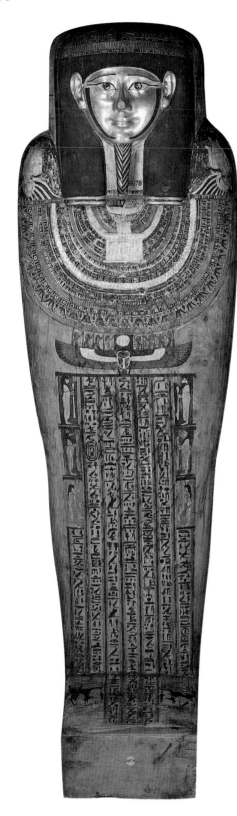

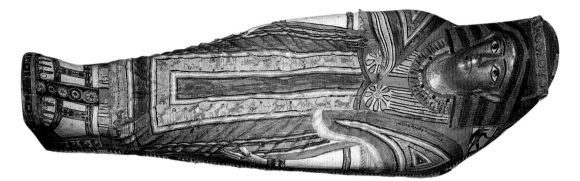

where on the lid and a gigantic figure on the inside floor (falcon-headed Osiris-Sokaris was particularly popular). During the Ptolemaic Period (after 305 BC) many coffins wore a pectoral plate and a huge multi-colour floral collar with falcon-headed terminals. The most frequently-occurring figured scene in the welter of hieroglyphs showed the mummy lying on a bier. Some coffins of the period are characterised by being grossly broad in proportion to their height; others have the head sunk into the chest and are almost cylindrical in section. Everything which could be was gilded, gaudily painted or both.

During the early first century AD a form of coffin made from moulded cartonnage and stucco showing the deceased in daily dress and painted in glaringly bright colours, especially shocking pink, was popular with some Greek inhabitants of Egypt. Other foreigners came to prefer a traditional mummiform cartonnage case decorated with Egyptian funerary themes into which a most un-Egyptian portrait panel was inserted.

65 Opposite, left *Inner wooden coffin of the Theban priest Hornedjitef with characteristic gilded face, pectoral and falcon collar. Ptolemaic Period, c.230 BC. Height 1.94 m (6 ft 4 1/2 in).*

66 Opposite, right *Wooden inner coffin of Horsanakht, bought from stock but with the text added later in crude hieratic. The decoration and high shoulders are characteristic of the period. Kharga Oasis. Ptolemaic Period, c.250 BC. Height 1.84 m (6 ft 1/2 in).*

67 Top *Gilded and painted cartonnage and stucco coffin moulded to fit the mummy of the woman Tamin and showing her wearing daily dress. Akhmim. Graeco-Roman Period, c.150 BC to AD 50. Height 1.50 m (4 ft 11 in).*

68 Right *Painted and gilded stucco mummy case with an epitaph in Greek naming Artemidorus and incorporating an encaustic portrait of the deceased. Hawara. Roman Period, early second century AD. Height 1.67 m (5 ft 5 3/4 in).*

Chapter Five | Funerals, Tombs and Burial Equipment

Although a nest of coffins and a stone sarcophagus afforded the mummy some physical protection, the greatest safeguard against destruction was the tomb itself, the destination of every funeral. Throughout Egyptian history there were basically only three types of tomb: the mastaba, the pyramid and the rock-cut tomb. From the earliest dynasties the mastaba was built on the open desert plateau, at first as a tomb for royalty or commoners, later exclusively for non-royal burials. It had a rectangular ground-plan and it was the appearance of the slightly sloping walls and flat roof of the superstructure which led to the adoption of the name *mastaba*, the Arabic word for 'bench'. At first the burial chamber and store rooms beneath the mastaba, which was originally built of solid mud-brick, were barely below ground level but the burial chamber moved deeper underground as the superstructure, now built of stone, became honeycombed with rooms and corridors. After the funeral had taken place the shaft from the roof, the only link between the burial chamber and the outside world, was blocked up. Provisions to feed the spirits of the dead were originally placed before a stone stela set against the east face of the mastaba, but it was gradually moved back into the superstructure and incorporated into a False Door inset into the west wall of an inner room which thus became the chapel or offering room. Adjoining it was the room called the *serdab*, completely walled off except for a vertical slit, where the statue of the tomb owner was kept as a temporary home for his *Ka* before it emerged through the False Door to partake of the essence of the daily offerings. The walls of the chapel were covered with scenes of food production and offering which could magically sustain the *Ka* should real provisions fail. Throughout the Old and Middle Kingdoms courtiers' mastabas were built in streets around the pyramid of their king.

Appropriately, the first pyramid, the stone Step Pyramid of King Djoser at Saqqara (about 2650 BC), is scarcely more than six squared-off mastabas of diminishing size set one on top of the other. Nearly one hundred years later the first true pyramid with smooth sides was built for King Sneferu at north Dahshur. Then, for the next eight hundred years or so, the pyramid continued to be an exclusively royal burial place, although by the end it was much reduced in size compared with the giants of the Fourth Dynasty pharaohs at Giza, and was constructed of rubble and merely cased with stone. A pyramid did not stand alone, but was part of a complex of buildings on the Western Plateau. Within the pyramid enclosure, on its east side, stood the pyramid temple (equivalent to the mastaba chapel) which was in constant use for the daily rites for the dead king. From its entrance a causeway ran down to the valley temple which stood at the edge of the cultivation with access to water. This temple, built on a T-shaped plan, was a replica in stone of the embalming tent and was where the mummification of the dead king took place. After the royal mummy had been taken up the causeway to be interred within the pyramid, the valley temple had no function except to serve as a magnificent entrance to the whole pyramid complex.

Although the internal passages of the pyramid were blocked and its entrance hidden once the king had been interred, by the early New Kingdom probably not one pyramid of any importance remained unplundered. Pyramids were just too conspicuous and too great a temptation, in spite of the difficulties, to potential robbers who knew that they contained untold wealth; the Egyptians really did take everything with them when they died. Tuthmosis I (about 1520 BC) was the first king to be buried in a rock-cut tomb hidden away in a remote valley on the west bank at Thebes, a site now called the Valley of the Kings. So as to afford no clue to the location of the royal tombs the relevant funerary temples (equivalent to pyramid temples) where the daily ritual for the dead kings was performed were built miles away at the edge of the cultivation.

Royal rock-cut tombs of the New Kingdom (Dynasties 18 to 20) usually consisted of numerous corridors, pillared halls, staircases and chambers, sometimes running for hundreds of feet into the rock, all highly decorated with religious scenes and texts and figures of Pharaoh with his fellow gods. But rock-cut tombs had existed for non-royal dead in provincial cemeteries since the Old Kingdom, wherever the terrain was unsuitable for mastabas and the cliffs came close to the Nile. The burial chamber was underground and the rooms cut into the cliffs were used as the offering chapel, their walls decorated with colourful scenes of daily life and funerary themes, although in the workmen's tombs at Deir el-Medina it was only the underground chambers with vaulted roofs which were decorated, and then only with scenes of the afterlife. It was also at Thebes during the New Kingdom that an interesting architectural development occurred: the chapel roofs of private tombs were crowned by a sharply-pointed mud-brick pyramid, capped with a stone pyramidion. This marked the last appearance of the pyramid in Egypt, a sorry shadow of its former self, diminished and democratised for the benefit of non-royal dead. Until the end of Egyptian history commoners continued to be buried underground, usually beneath an offering place of one kind or another. Royalty, however, apart from the Nubian kings of the Twenty-fifth Dynasty who revived the tradition of pyramid-shaped tombs far to the south in the modern Sudan, preferred to be entombed within temple precincts, judging from the finds at Tanis and Herodotus' account of the burials of kings of the Twenty-sixth Dynasty.

Because most cemeteries were on the West Bank a funeral nearly always involved a crossing of the Nile. In New Kingdom representations, however, it is often very difficult to distinguish between the original journey made by the corpse to the embalming place and the funeral crossing on the day of burial. Fortunately, a series of drawings in an Old Kingdom tomb at Meir records the correct sequence of events. The corpse was transported with little ceremony in a simple rectangular coffin on a papyrus skiff accompanied only by embalmers and funerary

69 Following pages *General view of the Valley of the Kings. In the foreground, the entrance to the tomb of Tutankhamun. Immediately behind and to the right, the entrance to the tomb of Ramesses VI.*

70 *Wall painting in the tomb of the scribe Simut called Kyky showing the mummy already on board a boat during the funeral crossing. In fact the funeral cortège would have collected it from the embalming workshop on the West Bank on the way to the tomb. Theban tomb 409. Nineteenth Dynasty, c.1250 BC.*

priests who, once ashore, either tucked the coffin under their arms or bore it aloft on their shoulders to the embalming place. On the day of burial the funeral cortège crossed the Nile and collected the mummy from the embalmers on the way to the tomb. Yet in some New Kingdom representations of the funeral crossing, the mummy is already lying beneath a gaily decorated canopy on a boat among the flotilla carrying family and friends, priests and professional mourners, servants, offerings and grave goods. To complicate matters further another water journey is depicted in many tombs representing a symbolic visit to Abydos. When Osiris became pre-eminent as god of the dead everyone wished to be buried at his chief cult place, or at least that their mummy should visit it. Usually, of course, not even the latter was possible, so a wooden model of the mummy on a boat or a representation of the journey on the tomb wall (in which the deceased usually appears as a statue) had to serve

71 *Wooden model funerary boat on which is a mummy under a canopy accompanied by female mourners, probably a three-dimensional representation of the journey to Abydos. Twelfth Dynasty, 1850 BC. Length 66.7 cm (26 1/4 in).*

instead. Occasionally, yet another symbolic water journey, this time to the ancient delta city of Busiris, was also depicted.

Although there is a good deal of individual variation because the choice of details depicted, even the order in which they appear, seems to have been left to the tomb owner, a non-royal funeral during the New Kingdom always contained certain elements. The mummy usually lies inside a shrine-shaped open booth which is bedecked with funerary bouquets and mounted on a boat-shaped bier set on a sled drawn by oxen. In one instance mummy, booth and bier are carried on mourners' shoulders; in another, four mourners carry just the mummy tucked under their arms. By tradition, some mourners make a token show of pulling the sled

too, but most of the important guests walk together. Sometimes the grieving widow kneels beside the bier but the mummy is regularly attended by two female mourners impersonating Isis and Nephthys as the two kites who wheeled and screeched over the body of Osiris. A shrine or coffin-shaped panelled cover, often elaborately decorated with amuletic symbols, which in reality hid the mummy from profane eyes during the procession, is usually shown raised, for artistic convention in tomb scenes required that the mummy be seen to be present. A priest always walks in front of the bier sprinkling milk and wafting incense, and close behind follows the Canopic chest, dragged on a sled or carried aloft on attendants' shoulders.

Most of the procession, however, is taken up by servants. Some carry portable tables and trays piled high with food and flowers, jars of wine and jugs of beer, napkins and unguent cones for the feast after the

72-3 *Vignettes from the* Book of the Dead *papyrus of Any depicting his funeral procession and the Opening of the Mouth ceremony at the tomb. Nineteenth Dynasty, c.1250 BC. Height 8 cm (3 1/8 in).*

74 *Vignette depicting the Opening of the Mouth ceremony carried out on Hunefer's mummy from his* Book of the Dead *papyrus. Nineteenth Dynasty, c.1280 BC. Height 31.9 cm (12 1/2 in).*

burial. Others carry the possessions of the deceased which will be taken with him into the tomb. Beds, complete with mattress and headrest, chairs and stools with cushions, boxes and chests, kilts, wigs and sandals, walking sticks and staffs of office, wine jars and draw-neck bags, jewellery of every kind, mirrors, stone vessels and fans, gaming boards, tables and stands are depicted in tomb after tomb, balanced on heads, supported in arms, slung from poles or hung from any available elbow or strut. Sometimes, though, an individual touch creeps in: weapons, shields and a prancing horse yoked to a chariot for a soldier's burial, writing equipment for a scribe. Boxes full of *shabti*-figures, figurines of gods and kings, magical objects for the burial chamber, ritual implements for use during the last rites are borne along too and, by artistic licence, equipment already wrapped in place on the mummy like the gilded funerary mask, golden vulture and falcon collars, heart scarabs and amulets of stone and precious metal.

Somewhere in the procession, too, is the mysterious *tekenu* apparently representing a crouching man completely enveloped in a cloak and dragged along on a sled. Once he might have been a human sacrifice slain to take on the sins of the dead man, but by now his slaughter is only token. Elsewhere the *muu*-dancers, wearing only kilts and tall white headdresses resembling the crown of Upper Egypt, caper around and clap their hands above their heads. Low-grade priests dressed all in white with shaven heads attend the *Sem*-Priest, distinguished by a panther skin over his shoulder, who is in charge of the proceedings, and the Lector Priest keeps up a constant recital of prayers and spells from an unrolled papyrus. And over the whole procession would float the wails and screams of the professional mourners. Robed in pale blue (the colour of mourning), they beat their bared breasts, tear their hair, rake their cheeks with their nails and throw earth over themselves to show how sorely the deceased is missed: presumably they were paid by performance and not at fixed rates.

Of all the rituals performed for the deceased just before burial the most important was the Opening of the Mouth which restored to the wrapped mummy all its faculties and bodily functions so that the afterlife might be enjoyed to the full. Originally this was carried out in the Purification Tent, but by the New Kingdom the mummy is usually shown propped up on a heap of clean sand before the tomb chapel while the *Sem*-Priest, in the role of the deceased's son, prepares to use the ritual implements set out nearby and the Lector Priest reads out appropriate instructions from an open papyrus. Occasionally the moment at which the mummy is purified by streams of water and is about to be offered the foreleg cut from a still-bleating calf is depicted, but the full Opening of the Mouth ritual is more often shown being performed upon the tomb statue. After all, it too needed to be given life in order to act as a temporary home for the *Ka* or even as a substitute body should the mummy be destroyed. Khafre, builder of the second pyramid at Giza, had no less than twenty-three such statues, one for each of the twenty-six parts which were thought to comprise the human body (three parts come in pairs) and the Opening of the Mouth had to be performed on them twenty-six times (three statues were treated twice). The ritual involved touching the face of the statue or mummy with the forked *pesesh kaf*, the chisel, the adze and the rod ending in a snake's head. Offerings were made of natron, grains of incense, eye-paint, linen, food and drink and the all-important foreleg and bull's heart, and there were regular anointings with sacred oils and censings and libations, all accompanied by prescribed gestures and appropriate incantations.

75 *Opening of the Mouth equipment. Model wooden adze, Eighteenth Dynasty, c.1450 BC, length 9.8 cm (3 7/8 in); alabaster tablet with depressions for samples of the seven sacred oils named in the inscription, Old Kingdom, c.2300 BC, width 13.7 cm (5 5/12 in); set of model vessels and implements of crystal, schist and limestone inset into a limestone base, Old Kingdom, c.2300 BC, width 11.7 cm (4 3/5 in).*

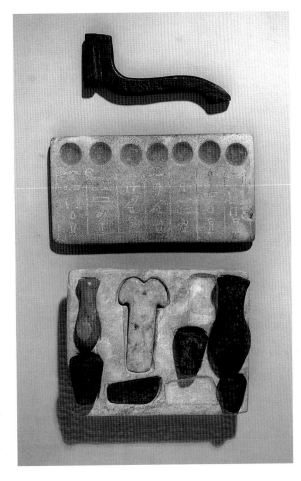

76 *Plaster-stiffened linen hypocephalus for setting beneath the mummy's head, bearing figures of the Canopic deities and sky-cow and an abbreviated version of Chapter 162 of the* Book of the Dead, *a spell to provide warmth. Ptolemaic Period, c.300 BC. Width 11.1 cm (4 3/8 in).*

Now the mummy could be placed in its nest of coffins, the Canopic chest set in its niche and the grave goods stacked round about. But before the burial chamber was sealed, final magical and protective aids were put in position. During the Late Period a flat disc made of bronze or plaster-stiffened linen called a hypocephalus was placed under the mummy's head and the spell upon it, Chapter 162 of the *Book of the Dead*, ensured that the deceased would be kept warm in the Other World. From the early Eighteenth Dynasty a rolled up copy of the *Book of the Dead* would be placed in the coffin or, later, in a hollowed-out plinth upon which stood a wooden figure of Ptah-Sokaris-Osiris, one of the forms of the god of the dead. The title *Book of the Dead* is given to a repertoire of nearly two hundred spells or chapters, written on papyrus and illustrated with vignettes, which were intended to help the dead pass through the perils of the Underworld and reach Heaven. Many of the spells are first found in the Middle Kingdom Coffin Texts, which were themselves based on the so-called Pyramid Texts, inscribed in Old Kingdom pyramids from the reign of Wenis onwards (about 2350 BC). No single papyrus contains all the chapters, but wealthy customers could at least choose which ones were included. Poorer customers bought a ready-written *Book of the Dead* and had their name added where gaps had been left for the purpose.

77 *Painted wooden Ptah-Sokaris-Osiris figure in which the funerary papyrus of the priestess Anhay was hidden. Late New Kingdom, c.1090 BC. Height 63.5 cm (2 ft 1 in).*

The vignette of Chapter 110 showed the Field of Reeds in the Other World where emmer, barley and flax grew as tall as a man, trees were laden with fruit and grain was stacked in heaps. But it was the dead who were expected to maintain this paradise of plenty by ploughing, sowing and reaping for all eternity. This is why *shabti*-figures of glazed composition, wood, stone, pottery, even bronze, wax or glass, came to be placed in the burial chamber. When they first appeared during the Middle Kingdom, *shabtis* were mummiform like the deceased, often carried amuletic signs and were inscribed with a prayer to provide food offerings. Their original symbolism is rather obscure; even the meaning of the word was soon forgotten by the Egyptians themselves, who eventually called them *ushabtis* or 'Answerers'. By the early New Kingdom, however, the little figures were clearly considered servants of the deceased who would carry out in place of their master all the hard agricultural work required

78 *Vignette depicting agricultural activities in the Field of Reeds illustrating Chapter 110 of the* Book of the Dead *of the scribe Nakht. The deceased is variously shown pulling flax, cutting emmer and barley, ploughing, adoring the heron of plenty and paddling a canoe. Eighteenth to Nineteenth Dynasties, c.1300–1290 BC. Height 30 cm (11 3/4 in).*

79 Shabti *figures: painted lime-stone Rensenb, c.1750 BC; wooden peg Djehuty, c.1600 BC, height 10 cm (3 ¹¹/₁₂ in); painted limestone unnamed priestess, c.1375 BC; gilded steatite Monthu, c.1375 BC, height 11.6 cm (4 ⁹/₁₆ in); wooden king Sety I, c.1279 BC; steatite Sunur and* Ba, *c.1275 BC, height 21.4 cm (8 ²/₅ in); glazed composition Pypypu, c.1250 BC, height 14.2 cm (5 ⁹/₁₆ in); glazed composition Bakwerner, c.1250 BC, height 13.1 cm (5 ¹/₆ in); painted alabaster king Ramesses VI, c.1136 BC, height 11.4 cm (4 ¹/₂ in); painted wooden Merenset, c.1100 BC, height 17.7 cm (7 in); glazed composition overseer queen Henttawy, c.1050 BC; bronze king Psusennes I, c.1000 BC, height 7.6 cm (3 in); glazed composition Horkhebyt, c.650 BC, height 15.4 cm (6 ¹/₁₆ in); glazed composition Psamtek, c.550 BC; glazed composition Padiwesir, c.250 BC, height 13.8 cm (5 ⁵/₁₂ in).*

of him in the Other World. They were equipped with a pick, hoe or adze, a seed bag or water pots and were inscribed with Chapter 6 of the *Book of the Dead*, the *shabti* formula: 'O *shabti*, if the deceased is called upon to do any of the work required there in the necropolis at any time . . . you shall say "Here I am, I will do it." ' By the end of the New Kingdom anyone who could afford to do so might have 401 *shabtis* stored in colourfully decorated boxes: 365 mummiform *shabtis* each served for one day of the year and over them were set 36 overseer *shabtis* wearing daily dress and carrying whips to make sure there was no slacking.

Much of Egyptian funerary practice was aimed at providing sustenance in the tomb for fear that the spirit forms which survived death would perish without it. Although tomb walls were covered with scenes of food production and offering and formulae which could magically feed the *Ka* should real offerings fail, as an extra safeguard actual food and drink were often placed in the burial chamber. Tutankhamun had no less than 116 baskets of fruit, 40 jars of wine, many boxes of roast duck and a number of loaves and cakes with him. During the First Intermediate

80 Left *Painted wooden* shabti-*box and* shabtis *of the Theban priestess Henutmehit showing her before the Canopic deities. Nineteenth Dynasty, c.1250* BC. *Height 34 cm (13 5/12 in).*

81 Below *Wooden model servants making bread. One kneads the dough, the other shields his face from the fire which he stokes with a poker. Asyut. Middle Kingdom, c.2000* BC. *Length 42 cm (16 1/2 in).*

Period and early Middle Kingdom, in order to supplement wall scenes or even replace them completely, some non-royal burials were equipped with whole teams of wooden model servants shown at work, especially tasks connected with the provision of food and drink such as brewing, baking and butchering, or bringing every kind of food offering. Even model houses which were placed in

82 Left *Pottery soul-house with a window, a waterspout and stairs to the roof upon which is a wind-vent to catch the breeze. Models of provisions are represented in the forecourt. Middle Kingdom, c.1900 BC. Height at back 17.3 cm (6 4/5 in).*

83 Below *Food placed in the burial chamber to provide sustenance for the dead: a reedwork table laden with cooked duck and coarse bread, height 21.8 cm (8 3/5 in). Flat loaves on a woven fibre dish; dom-palm fruit; a bowl of sun-dried fish. All New Kingdom, c.1450-1240 BC.*

contemporary tombs as an alternative dwelling for the *Ka*, and are accordingly termed soul-houses, always have tiny representations of provisions in the forecourt.

Some types of funerary equipment are associated with burials of a particular period. During the Old Kingdom quite naturalistically carved stone heads were placed near the entrance to the burial chamber. These are called 'reserve heads' because they probably served as a substitute for the head of the deceased, should his body be destroyed. Ivory wands shaped like boomerangs and carved with a frieze of gods and demons offered protection to the dead during the Middle Kingdom. Some New Kingdom burials contained an Osiris bed, a box in the shape of an outline Osiris which was filled with Nile mud planted with grain which sprouted in the darkness of the tomb and, presumably, afforded the dead the same capability of new birth.

Now, at last, the burial chamber could be sealed forever, but only after weapons and other such possessions which, in hostile hands, could harm the dead had been ritually damaged and magic bricks and figurines had been set around the coffin as illustrated by Chapter 151 of the *Book of the Dead*. Then, while mourners ate the funerary feast at the tomb door, the pots containing refuse embalming material, required by the dead but too ritually unclean to be stored within the burial chamber itself, were buried nearby.

84 *Vignette illustrating Chapter 151 of the* Book of the Dead *of the Theban priestess Muthetepti, representing a plan of the burial chamber. The mummy and its* Ba *tended by Anubis are surrounded by protective amulets and deities including a* djed, *a* shabti *and a flame, Isis and Nephthys and the Four Sons of Horus. Additional* Bas *are shown in adoration. Twentieth Dynasty, c.1100 BC. Height 31 cm (12 ¹/₅ in).*

Chapter Six | Animal and Historical Mummies

As an interesting sidelight on embalming much has been learned about ancient Egyptian insect and small animal life from the bodies of creatures for which the mummy and its wrappings became a grave. Flies, beetles and cockroaches which began feeding on the corpse during its treatment were embalmed themselves when hot resin was applied; crickets and small lizards were sometimes trapped on the sticky surface of the bandages and wrapped in with the mummy. In one instance, lazy and disrespectful embalmers dropped the body of a dead mouse together with used linen swabs onto a mummy's knees and hid them with the next layer of wrappings. After the mummy of King Amenophis I had been stripped by tomb robbers searching for objects of precious metal it was rewrapped during the Twenty-first Dynasty on the orders of the Theban High Priest of Amun and, as a final gesture, a garland of delphiniums was placed on its chest. When the coffin was opened nearly three thousand years later their pungent fragrance flooded the room and the body of a wasp, attracted by the same scent all those centuries before, was found trapped like a fly in amber among the

85 *Mummified animals: an ibis mummy characteristically conical in outline, Abydos, length 37.5 cm (14 3/4 in); mummy of a dog, Abydos, height 33.5 cm (13 1/5 in); two falcon mummies bandaged together, Thebes, height 25 cm (9 5/6 in). All Roman Period, after 30 BC.*

unguents which had been poured over the mummy just before the lid was closed.

The Egyptians did, of course, deliberately embalm the bodies of very many creatures because they believed that most of their gods and goddesses were able to appear on earth in the form of a sacred animal. Amun, the king of the gods, might disguise himself as a ram or goose; a cow might really be Hathor or Isis; Sobk lurked in the form of a crocodile; Horus soared heavenwards as a falcon. Originally, though, not all members of a particular species were held sacred – after all, most geese were bred to be eaten. It was only those individual animals lucky enough to be chosen to live in a temple precinct as the earthly representative of the temple deity who were spared to live a life of luxury and were embalmed and buried with due ceremony when they died. By the Late Period, however, the idea seems to have got out of hand: any species which could be considered sacred was considered so, each and every member of it. Thus mummies have survived of snakes, fish, shrew-mice, gazelles and beetles as well as baboons, falcons, crocodiles and dogs. Thousands of animals may even have been bred purely to supply bodies to be embalmed for the flourishing trade which provided sacred animal mummies for pious pilgrims to dedicate and bury, at a price, at important cult centres. At Saqqara alone an estimated four million embalmed ibises have been found, each in a conical pottery canister, stacked from floor to ceiling in dozens of rooms off underground corridors. Last century hundreds of tons of mummified cats were shipped from their find-place at Beni Hasan in Middle Egypt to the English port of Liverpool to be turned into fertiliser.

But throughout Egyptian history some individual animals during their lifetime were considered to be the living incarnation of a god. Obviously, there could only be one such animal at any one time. Perhaps the most famous is the Apis bull, earthly manifestation of the god Ptah, whose history goes back to the very beginning of the Dynastic Period. The Apis was selected from all other bulls because of particular markings on his body. Once chosen he was installed with great ceremony in quarters next to the temple of Ptah at Memphis, attended by his own servants and a harem of cows, visited by pious worshippers and only appearing in public at great festivals to

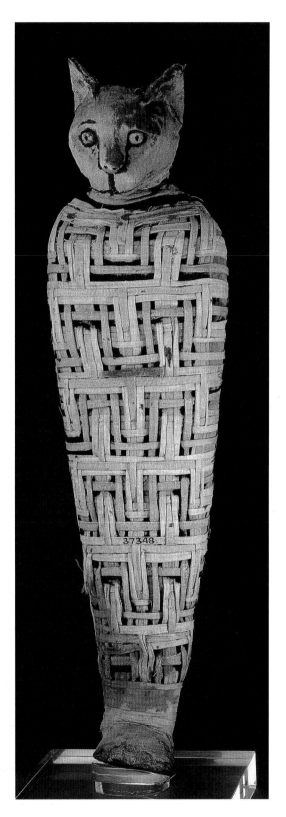

86 Intricately bandaged mummy of a cat The arrangement of the wrappings in geometrical patterns is characteristic of the period. Abydos. Roman Period, after 30 BC. Height 46 cm (18 ¹/₈ in).

deliver oracles. The cow who had borne him was also held in great honour, for she was the mother of a god. Until the end of the New Kingdom it is probable that when the Apis died his body was ritually eaten, but by the Late Period he was embalmed with all the pomp of a pharaoh, except that a full-sized bull required rather more treatment than a human corpse. The huge alabaster embalming tables where the dead bulls received their natron treatment can still be seen at the site of Memphis. The Serapeum is the underground catacomb at Saqqara where they were buried, equipped with bullheaded *shabtis*, in granite sarcophagi weighing more than 60 tons.

But nearly all the Apis burials were robbed or destroyed by rampaging Christians, so it is the burials of another bull, the Buchis sacred to Monthu at Hermonthis near Thebes, which have thus far provided most information. However, a recently studied demotic text of late Ptolemaic date which concerns the step-by-step embalming of an Apis bull has provided much confirmatory and even new evidence. The entrails of the Buchis were not removed through an incision but *per anum*: bronze instruments identical with enemas and retractors used by modern vets were found among embalming equipment in their burial place. The bull was elaborately bandaged in a reclining position with its legs bent beneath it, and was attached to a base board by bandages passed through metal clamps. Inlaid eyes were set into the gilded plaster mask which covered the head and a headdress with two tall plumes inlaid with glass above a sun disc was fixed between the horns.

Desiccation by natron was not the only method of embalming practised in Egypt. The body of Alexander the Great was reputedly preserved in honey and exhibited in a glass coffin so that it might be seen afloat in the sticky substance. This gives a ghastly ring of truth to the story related by the Arab historian Abd el-Latif, writing about 1200 AD, concerning treasure-seekers of his acquaintance who found an unopened pot of honey near the pyramids. They dipped their bread into it quite happily until they noticed a floating hair which was discovered to be still attached to the head of a perfectly preserved child's body.

The survival of some mummies has helped to bring dry historical facts to life. When the Theban prince Mentuhotep II finally reunited Egypt in about 2040 BC after more than a century of civil war much of the fighting must have centred around fortresses of the type depicted in contemporary tombs. Mute

87 Opposite *Elaborately bandaged mummy of a calf. Thebes, Roman Period, after 30 BC. Max. height 45 cm (17 3/4 in).*

88 *Sandstone stela from the Bucheum showing the Roman emperor Diocletian worshipping the Buchis bull which is represented as an elaborately bandaged mummy. Armant, 288 AD. Height 67 cm (26 3/8 in).*

89 *Head of the mummy of king Seqenenre II showing the wounds from which he eventually died. From the royal cache of mummies at Deir el-Bahri, Thebes. Seventeenth Dynasty, c.1570 BC. (Cairo Museum.)*

90 *Small wrapped mummy found in the coffin of the Theban priestess Maatkare, thought to be a baby, now known to be a baboon. From the royal cache of mummies at Deir el-Bahri, Thebes. Twenty-first Dynasty, c.1050 BC. Height 41 cm (16 1/8 in). (Cairo Museum.)*

testimony is provided by the bodies of sixty of his archers buried in a single chamber near his temple at Deir el-Bahri. They had all been shot by missiles raining from above, a few who had been only wounded had been finished off by a blow to the head, and all the bodies had been fed upon by birds of prey. Clearly they had been shot by defenders on ramparts, and victory was not immediate since the enemy had killed the wounded and prevented the recovery of the bodies for some time: perhaps they were the casualties of the last battle of the civil war.

The mummy of King Seqenenre II (about 1580 BC) is a ghastly sight. There is a gaping hole in his right temple exposing the brain. Other blows have smashed his cheek-bone and nose and there is a stab wound below the left ear, and in his death agony he has bitten through his tongue. Surely he died in battle and because his body was in an advanced state of decomposition before it was treated, he cannot have died in victory. The hero of the Sallier I papyrus (EA 10185) is a Theban prince called Seqenenre who is goaded into rebelling against his Hyksos overlord. The end of the story is lost but it was not until the reign of Amosis, the second successor of Seqenenre II, that the Hyksos were finally driven from Egypt. Surely Seqenenre II must have been the prince who began the war of independence but died heroically before he could finish it. Yet, most intriguingly, recent re-examination of the mummy has suggested that an original theory – Seqenenre was assassinated – might have some weight after all. There is clear evidence of new bone growth in the worst head wound which proves the king survived his injuries for some time but would certainly have been paralysed. A nation on a war-footing required an able-bodied leader; an assassin's blow would have solved the problem.

Other mummies pose fresh puzzles. Maatkare, daughter of the High Priest Pinudjem I (about 1050 BC), held the highest of all female priestly offices, God's Wife of Amun, which demanded celibacy. Yet with her mummy was found a tiny wrapped body which was always thought to be that of a baby. Needless to say, this led to all kinds of speculation about the private life of Maatkare. Recently, however, X-rays have revealed that the baby is really the mummy of a baboon. But why was it placed in the coffin of Maatkare, especially when examination of her body has shown that she did, in fact, die during or just after childbirth? Was it a substitute baby for a child who survived?

Among the cache of royal mummies found at Deir el-Bahri was a body placed in a plain wooden coffin with no identification whatsoever. Even more curiously, it was wrapped in a sheepskin, a material which Herodotus says was considered ritually unclean, a fact confirmed by a passage in the Egyptian text called the Wanderings of Sinuhe. As an eye-witness called Mathey recorded when the body was unwrapped: 'It is difficult to give an accurate description of the expression of the face thus laid bare. I can only say that no countenance has ever more faithfully recreated a picture of such affecting and hideous agony. His features, horribly distorted, show that the wretched man must have been deliberately asphyxiated — most probably by being buried alive.' The mouth is open in a soundless scream, the stomach painfully contracted, the arms tightly bound down by the sides and the legs tied together. He undoubtedly died in convulsions but did the embalmers really set to work on him while he was still alive? No attempt has been made to remove the internal organs and natron had only been applied next to the skin and among the bandages. The presence of the body in a royal cache suggests that the unknown man was a prince. But the summary embalming and the disrespect shown by the use of the sheepskin and plain coffin suggest that he had committed some unforgivable offence. At the end of the reign of Ramesses III (about 1153 BC) a harem conspiracy aimed to set a concubine's son on the throne instead of the rightful heir. The plot was discovered and the prince who had been implicated seems to have been allowed to commit suicide, perhaps by taking poison. Could the unmummified body belong to that very prince, or another whose conspiracy also failed?

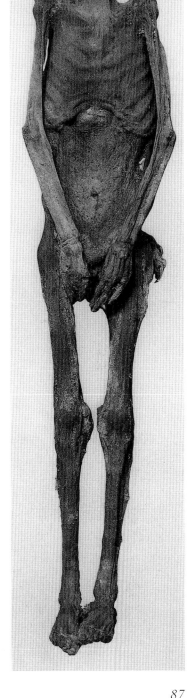

91 *Unmummified body of an unknown man, presumably a prince, found wrapped in sheepskin in an unmarked coffin From the royal cache of mummies at Deir el-Bahri, Thebes. New Kingdom. Height 1.71 m (5 ft 7 5/16 in). (Cairo Museum.)*

Chapter Seven | Mummies and Europe

Presumably because of the confusion between the appearance of bitumen and the resin-impregnated flesh of Late Period bodies, both termed '*mummiya*', a stomach-churning business developed in ground-up mummy as a drug. As early as the twelfth century AD an Arab physician called El-Magar prescribed it for patients and by the sixteenth century it was a stock ingredient in the apothecary shops of Europe. The French monarch Francis I never went anywhere without a pouch of mummy mixed with pulverised rhubarb to be administered immediately if he fell or was wounded because of its supposed power to staunch blood. The philosopher Francis Bacon swore by it, but Ambrose Paré, an eminent French surgeon, was one of the few whose voices were raised against 'this wicked kind of drogge'. In fact, the taking of powdered mummy caused violent nausea which presumably took the patient's mind off his original ailment.

So brisk was the trade in mummies to Europe that even after ransacking tombs and catacombs there just were not enough ancient Egyptian bodies to meet demand. And so fake mummies were fabricated from the corpses of executed criminals, the aged, the poor and those who had died from hideous diseases, by burying them in the sand like Ginger or stuffing them with bitumen and exposing them to the sun. As doubts grew about the effectiveness of the drug the export of mummies was finally brought to an end by the Turkish rulers of Egypt who imposed hefty fines on traffickers in mummy. Their main aim was to raise money, but they also believed that some fiendish Christian plot must lie behind the never-ending European demand for ancient Egyptian bodies. Yet a mere fifty years ago a French archaeologist reported continued use of mummy as medicine in Egypt and genuine powdered mummy can apparently still be bought for forty dollars an ounce from a New York pharmacy catering to the needs of the occult trade.

Curiously enough, at about the same time as the traffic in mummies died the myth of the mummy's curse first made its appearance: the earliest record of a ghost story involving a mummy is dated to 1699 and recounted by a Frenchman called Louis Penicher in his book entitled *Traité des embaumements selon les anciens et les modernes*. This was a full century before the decipherment of hieroglyphs when translations of Egyptian texts provided writers of the macabre and, more recently, makers of horror films, with a whole new subject. And once suggested, the idea of a mummy wreaking vengeance from beyond the tomb has never lost its popular appeal. The Curse of Tutankhamun was a jour-

92 *Painted and modelled wooden mummy board or coffin lid of an unnamed Theban priestess, known incorrectly as 'the unlucky mummy'. It is reputed to have been on the Titanic in 1912, although it has only left the Museum premises once (in 1990) since it entered the Egyptian Collection in 1889. Twenty-first Dynasty, c.1050 BC Height 1.62 m (5 ft 3 13/16 in).*

nalistic invention but books are still written about it. That the British Museum's unlucky mummy (EA 22542) is not a mummy but a perfectly harmless coffin lid or mummy board of an unnamed lady of the Twenty-first Dynasty which has never brought ill-luck or caused death, and certainly had nothing to do with the sinking of the Titanic, has not prevented its fictitious history being repeated by writer after writer.

Yet the introduction of the supernatural is quite unnecessary for mummies to arouse wonderment. Is it not a great enough marvel that through the embalmer's skill we can look upon the actual features of kings who ruled fifteen centuries before the birth of Christ, and commoners who lived when the pyramids were new?

Further Reading

Maurice Bucaille, *Mummies of the Pharaohs*, New York 1988

Aidan & Eve Cockburn (eds), *Mummies, Disease and Ancient Cultures*, Cambridge 1980

Warren R. Dawson & P.M.K. Gray, *Catalogue of Egyptian Antiquities in the British Museum. 1: Mummies and Human Remains*, London 1968

Joyce M. Filer, *Disease*, London 1995

Renate Germer, *Mummies, Life after Death in Ancient Egypt*, Munich 1997

James Hamilton-Paterson & Carol Andrews, *Mummies: Death and Life in Ancient Egypt*, London 1978

James E. Harris & Kent R. Weeks, *X-Ray Atlas of the Royal Mummies*, Chicago 1980

Ange-Pierre Leca, *The Cult of the Immortal*, London 1980

John H. Taylor, *Unwrapping a Mummy*, London 1995

The Dynasties of Egypt

Early Dynastic Period
(DYNASTIES I-II)
First Dynasty
*c.*3100-2890 BC
Second Dynasty
*c.*2890-2686 BC

Old Kingdom
(DYNASTIES III-VIII)
Third Dynasty
*c.*2686-2613 BC
Fourth Dynasty
*c.*2613-2494 BC
Fifth Dynasty
*c.*2494-2345 BC
Sixth Dynasty
*c.*2345-2181 BC
Seventh Dynasty
*c.*2181-2173 BC
Eighth Dynasty
*c.*2173-2160 BC

First Intermediate Period
(DYNASTIES IX-X)
Ninth Dynasty
*c.*2160-2130 BC
Tenth Dynasty
*c.*2130-2040 BC

Middle Kingdom
(DYNASTIES XI-XII)
Eleventh Dynasty
*c.*2133-1991 BC
Twelfth Dynasty
*c.*1991-1786 BC

Second Intermediate Period
(DYNASTIES XIII-XVII)
Thirteenth Dynasty
*c.*1786-1633 BC
Fourteenth Dynasty
*c.*1715-1650 BC

Fifteenth Dynasty
(Hyksos)
*c.*1648-1450 BC
Sixteenth Dynasty
*c.*1650-1550 BC
Seventeenth Dynasty
*c.*1650-1550 BC

New Kingdom
(DYNASTIES XVIII-XX)
Eighteenth Dynasty
*c.*1550-1295 BC
Nineteenth Dynasty
1295-1186 BC
Twentieth Dynasty
1186-1070 BC

Third Intermediate Period
(DYNASTIES XXI-XXV)
Twenty-first Dynasty
*c.*1069-945 BC
Twenty-second Dynasty
*c.*945-715 BC
Twenty-third Dynasty
*c.*818-715 BC
Twenty-fourth Dynasty
*c.*727-715 BC
Twenty-fifth Dynasty
*c.*747-656 BC

Late Dynastic Period
(DYNASTIES XXVI-XXX)
Twenty-sixth Dynasty
*c.*664-525 BC
Twenty-seventh Dynasty
*c.*525-404 BC
Twenty-eighth Dynasty
*c.*404-399 BC
Twenty-ninth Dynasty
*c.*399-380 BC
Thirtieth Dynasty
*c.*380-343 BC

Persian Kings
*c.*343-332 BC

Macedonian Kings
c.332-305 BC

Graeco-Roman Period
c.305 BC/AD 323
PTOLEMAIC KINGS
c.305-30 BC
ROMAN EMPERORS
c.30 BC/AD 395

Index to the Collection Numbers of Objects Illustrated

Index

Photographic Acknowledgements

The author and publishers are grateful to the following for permission to reproduce photographs:

Cairo Museum 6, 7, 10, 15, 22, 89, 90, 91

Hildesheim Museum 12

Figs 9, 10, 20, 69, 70 are the author's copyright. All other photographs have been provided by the Photographic Service of the British Museum and the work of Peter Hayman and James Rossiter is particularly acknowledged.